HORIZON

JULY, 1961 · VOLUME III, NUMBER 6

OTTO NELSON—PRIVATE COLLECTION

HORIZON

JULY, 1961 · *VOLUME III, NUMBER 6*

HORIZON is published every two months by American Heritage Publishing Co., Inc. Executive and editorial offices: 551 Fifth Ave., New York 17, N.Y. HORIZON welcomes contributions but can assume no responsibility for unsolicited material.

All correspondence about subscriptions should be addressed to: HORIZON Subscription Office, 379 West Center St., Marion, Ohio.

Single Copies: $4.50
Annual Subscriptions: $21.00 in the U.S. & Can.
$22.00 elsewhere

An annual index is published every September, priced at $1. HORIZON is also indexed in the *Readers Guide to Periodical Literature.*

Title registered U.S. Patent Office
Second-class postage paid at New York, N.Y.

COVER: When Francesco Guardi painted the Piazza San Marco late in the eighteenth century (in a painting of which this is a detail), Venice had long since developed a way of life that was unique. "It resembled," said the Italian historian Pompeo Molmenti, "the life of a great family that never left the house; the canals and *calli* were its corridors, the little squares its anterooms, and the larger squares its salons." The problem of today's cities is to recover this intimate quality, as Lewis Mumford points out in his new book *The City in History.* A pictorial treatment of the theme of Mr. Mumford's book, coupled with passages from it, begins on page 32. Guardi's *Piazza San Marco* is in the Metropolitan Museum of Art, Bequest of Mary Stillman Harkness, 1950.

FRONTISPIECE: Maharajah Man Singh of Marwar is out for a spin with his wives in his flower-decked *zula,* the hand-propelled, thousand-year-old Indian forerunner of the modern Ferris wheel. Wearing his emerald and pearl crown, the ruler (upper left) sips wine with his favorite wife and small son, who is almost lost in the sweep of her bell-shaped skirt. The other wives borne aloft in the *zula,* gossip and gesture to the tinkle of swinging bells and the rhythmic snapping of fingers from those below. A peaceful scene—but one of frustration for British officials who had long been delayed by such indulgences of the periodically mad Maharajah in their attempts to arbitrate the widespread civil wars that beset northwest India during much of his reign (1803–43). This Rajput painting by an unknown artist was commissioned by Man Singh in about 1830.

By RENE DUBOS

Goya's The Sleep [or Dream] of Reason *was prophetic in vision*

The Dream of Reason

Francis Bacon called scientists to the great task of creating Utopia. Their success has been so complete that it threatens disaster. One of their modern spokesmen now bids them consider the responsibility of Science to Man

Today, as every day, I have heard of ugly congested cities with polluted atmosphere; of planes loaded with youths colliding in mid-air; of overpopulated continents and starving populations; of mechanized, regimented, and dehumanized life; of brainwashing and nuclear warfare. As a member of the scientific community, I am awed by the thought that these social nightmares are to a large extent the products of industrial civilization—born out of science. And there comes to mind an etching by Goya, the central plate of his *Caprichos* series. Reproduced opposite, it shows a man sprawled across his desk, daydreaming or alseep, his head on his arms. Bats, owls, and a witch's cat surround him as in a nightmare. On the side of the desk are inscribed the words *"El sueño de la razon produce monstruos."*

I had assumed that this caption meant that the *sleep* of reason produces monsters. For, indeed, errors and superstitions readily take over and generate loathsome creatures when reason is asleep. It is more likely, however, that the caption refers not to sleep but to the undisciplined *dreams* of reason. To Aldous Huxley the etching means that "reason may intoxicate itself, as it did during the French Revolution." At that time reason engaged in daydreams of endless and inevitable progress, of utopias to be reached through the easy road of political liberty and more advanced technology.

Like Goya—for he himself is the dreamer sprawled over the desk in the etching—I recall that men of goodwill and of reason in all ages have believed that the problems of the world would soon be solved by science, the very science which instead has engendered some of the monsters that threaten us today.

The scientific revolution which began yielding its fruits during the seventeenth century can be traced in large part to the writings of one person: Francis Bacon. His place in the history of science is unique because his influence was exerted through words rather than deeds. He did not add to knowledge but became the prophet of scientific civilization.

It would be useless to tell once more the life history of Francis Bacon—Baron Verulam and Viscount St. Albans—who was born in London on January 22, 1561, and who died there on April 9, 1626. But it is of direct relevance to our theme that in addition to his interest in science, he was heavily involved in political activities of the most practical sort, an expert on legal matters, a writer of essays, and such a master of the English language that there are still some today who believe that he was the true author of Shakespeare's writings. His sense of practicalities and his extraordinary genius for literary expression were the main factors in determining his role in the subsequent history of science.

Bacon recognized, of course, that important contributions to science had been made in the past, and that still more were being made by his contemporaries. But he believed that on the whole, scientific scholarship had been conducted in a wasteful manner, contributing little to factual knowledge and even less to the improvement of the human condition.

Bacon based his scientific philosophy on the Christian dogma of Original Sin. While man had lost at the same time the state of innocence and his dominion over the external world, Bacon believed that these losses could be repaired to some extent on earth. Man could recover Adam's original state of happiness on the one hand by religious faith, on the other by the cultivation of science.

How can mankind use science to recapture the dominion over nature that was lost by the Fall? First we must shake off, according to Bacon, our intellectual bondage to the ancients, for they have so completely dominated our thoughts heretofore as to paralyze action. There is no doubt, of course, that "the ancients proved themselves in everything that turns on wit and abstract meditation, wonderful men. . . ." "Unfortunately," Bacon says, "that wisdom which we have derived principally from the Greeks is but like the boyhood of knowledge, and has the characteristic property of boys: it can talk, but it cannot generate; for it is fruitful of controversies but barren of works."

Moreover, what has come down to us from the past, in particular the teachings of Plato and Aristotle, is the least valuable part of ancient knowledge and wisdom, because it is the most superficial. "Time is like a river, which has brought down to us things light and puffed up, while those which are weighty and solid have sunk. . . ."

The greatest evil that we have inherited from the ancients is that their approach to knowledge is more conducive to talk than to action. "They had made the quiescent principles, *wherefrom*, and not the moving principles, *whereby* things are produced, the object of their contemplation and inquiry. The former tend to discourse, the latter to works."

Our most important task, then, said Bacon, is to discover how things work rather than to answer questions about their origin. Thus, he was convinced that man can achieve new things and improve the world only if he gives up haphazard observation and experimentation. He must formulate far-reaching goals and organize efforts in a more subtle and systematic way. Bacon recognized that not all experiments could be expected to lead immediately to practical results. Indeed, scientists should be willing to carry out "a variety of experiments, which are of no use in themselves, but simply serve to discover causes and axioms; which I call *experimenta lucifera,* experiments of light, to distinguish them from those which I call *fructifera,* experiments of fruit."

It is clear that he did not advocate a formula of science limited to the mere heaping-up of experimental data. Nowhere do the subtleness of his mind and the richness of Elizabethan language appear more brilliantly than in these famous sentences: "The men of experiment are like the ant; they only collect and use; the reasoners resemble spiders, who make cobwebs out of their own substance. But the bee takes a middle course, it gathers its material from the flowers of the garden and of the field, but transforms and digests it by a power of its own." Clearly, to be effective, the scientist

Now it can be said that it is possible to achieve almost anything we want—so great is the effectiveness of technology based on the experimental method. Thus, the main issue for scientists and for society as a whole is now to decide *what* to do among all the things that could be done and should be done. Unless scientists are willing to give hard thought—indeed, their hearts—to this latter aspect of their social responsibilities, they may find themselves someday in the position of the Sorcerer's Apprentice, unable to control the forces they have unleashed. And they may have to confess, like Captain Ahab in *Moby Dick,* that all their methods are sane, their goal mad.

—FROM THIS ARTICLE

had to resemble the bee, industrious but also imaginatively selective, in order to be truly creative.

Probably as a form of protest against the social neglect of science, Bacon depicted in the last of his writings, *The New Atlantis,* a utopian society guided by a community of scholars who devoted themselves entirely to scientific research, to the organization of knowledge, and to the pursuit of wisdom. In the words of their leader, "The end of our foundation is the knowledge of causes, and secret motions of things; and the enlarging of the bounds of human empire, to the effecting of all things possible." Thus did Francis Bacon, Lord of Verulam, Lord Chancellor of England, symbolize in Salomon's House his ideal of the scientific way of life, and in the utopian New Atlantis his concept of a society intelligently ruled by scientific philosophers.

Bacon's significance in history is thus to have blown the clarion call which awakened Europeans to the fact that science could completely transform society. He emphasized that in the past the applications of knowledge to the practical affairs of man had not been systematic but instead in the nature of stunts, accidental in occurrence, and kept secret if possible. In contrast, he preached a general method by which problems could be solved at will, thus permitting a progressive and continuously increasing mastery over nature through the systematic and uninterrupted pursuit of knowledge. He appears as the first statesman whose aim it was to organize human life in terms of a master plan framed by scientific thought. Unknowingly, William Harvey had characterized Bacon's greatness in saying that he wrote on science "like a Lord Chancellor"—in other words, like a great statesman of science.

It was the richness and convincing beauty of Bacon's language that made the world at large take notice of scientific knowledge as an instrument of power and of social growth, thus launching us on the road that we are still traveling today. No one questions any longer the fact that science is increasing the dominion of man over nature. This does not mean, of course, that man will recover through scientific technology the happiness that Adam knew before the Fall, as Bacon hoped. But Bacon certainly contributed to the modern world its most characteristic aspect and its most lasting illusion when he created his utopia of happiness based on application of scientific knowledge.

The revolutionary advances of the past two centuries suggest that almost any problem of human welfare can be solved if it is properly formulated and if its solution is diligently pursued. As a student of experimental medicine, I take it for granted that progress can be made in the control of any disease to which we address ourselves with enough energy. I feel confident, also, that physicists, chemists, and engineers can provide us with almost any kind of earthly good. I even believe that sociologists and politicians will find ways of improving relations among men, even though the result may be peace without love. From penicillin to supersonic flight, from the control of personality to space exploration, from elimination of child labor to universal suffrage, the twentieth century has been marked by many scientific and social achievements which are so startling as to dwarf the miracles of the legendary ages.

Despite all these modern miracles, there are many among us who speak regretfully of the old times and tend to place the golden age in the past rather than in the future. And, in fact, the many beautiful things that have come to us from the past are eloquent witnesses to a kind of happiness that we may well envy our ancestors: the lyrical outbursts of poets, the smiling angels in Gothic cathedrals, the glamourous feasts of the Renaissance, the gay celebrations of primitive country folk. How often we long for the profound and genuine happiness of yesteryear!

The disenchanted mood of today, of course, has its origin in the fact that happiness does not depend only upon comfort and contentment. Illiterates may well be contented and morons even more so—still more, perhaps, the proverbially contented cow or the well-fed household cat. But the further man evolves from his animal origin, the less happiness he can find in the mere removal of discomfort and in the satisfactions of the body. Every fulfillment, whatever its nature, is likely to create a new need and thus become a source of new dissatisfaction. The endless urge for some new experience, the tendency to look for goals beyond the attainable, are traits which differentiate man from other forms of life. These aspirations have led him to establish his dominance over the natural world, but certainly they are endlessly creating for him new problems which make of health and of happiness mirages that are ever receding into the future.

Until the end of the eighteenth century most of material civilization had been built out of practices evolved either empirically from the very experience of day-to-day life or from discoveries made by accident without prior scientific knowledge. In fact, much of science itself arose from these empirical achievements. Then, systematic scientific knowledge derived from laboratory experimentation rapidly overtook practical life, and scientists increasingly became the innovators and indeed the governors of human existence. It can be said that the scientific age began when, from toiling obscurely in the rear of the empirical procedures, science stepped forward and held up the torch in front. By the middle of the nineteenth century, scientific investigations undertaken in a search for pure knowledge began to suggest practical applications and inventions. Faraday's electromagnetic experiments led to the dynamo and other electromagnetic machines; Maxwell's studies of waves led to wireless telegraphy; Pasteur's work revolutionized fermentation industries and the practice of medicine, etc., etc.

As a result of this change, the business of everyday life is now carried out with the tools provided by science, and, more importantly, the very character of human existence is now molded by the products of scientific technology. While these facts are obvious and acknowledged by all—by those who deprecate them as well as by those who delight in them—it is not so well recognized that the direction of scientific effort during the past three centuries, and therefore the whole trend of modern life, has been markedly conditioned by an attitude fostered by the creators of utopias. They fostered the view that nature must be studied not so much to be understood as to be mastered and exploited by man.

The urge to control nature is probably the most characteristic aspect of Western civilization. It has not yet been proven, however, that this ideal is the best for human life. After all, great civilizations have been created in the past, and much profound happiness has been experienced, based on the philosophy that man must strive for harmony with the rest of nature instead of behaving toward it as a dominating lord and an exploiting master. It is much too early to be sure that Galileo, Watt, and Edison have contributed more lastingly to human advancement and happiness than have Socrates, Lao-tse, and Francis of Assisi.

The ethical problems posed by the utilization of knowledge are, of course, as old as mankind. But it is only during modern times that the question has become practically important as a result of the increasing effectiveness of scientific methods, and of the fact that science is now valued more for its social uses than as natural philosophy. In a recent address Ritchie Calder stated that "scientists leave their discoveries like foundlings on the doorstep of society. The step-parents do not know how to bring them up." Clearly, this attitude is no longer permissible now that scientific discoveries can have such far-reaching and lasting effects on human existence—indeed, on the fate of the human race. It is for society, of course, to decide what goals it wishes to reach and what risks it is willing to take. But it is the task of the scientific community to formulate as clearly as possible and to make public the probable consequences of any step that it takes and of any action that it advocates. In other words, the responsibility of the scientist does not stop when he has developed the knowledge and techniques that lead to a process or a product. Beyond that, he must secure and make public the kind of information on which the social body as a whole can base the value judgments that alone will decide long-range policies.

The relation of science to society has changed and become more complex during modern times. Three hundred years ago Bacon and his followers were justified in claiming that the important problem was to learn *how* to do things. There was then so little that could be done! Soon it became apparent that the most effective method of progress was to try to understand natural phenomena, their *whys* as much as theirs *hows*. Now it can be said that it is possible to achieve almost anything we want—so great is the effectiveness of technology based on the experimental method. Thus, the main issue for scientists and for society as a whole is now to decide *what* to do among all the things that could be done and should be done. Unless scientists are willing to give hard thought—indeed, their hearts—to this latter aspect of their social responsibilities, they may find themselves someday in the position of the Sorcerer's Apprentice, unable to control the forces they have unleashed. And they may have to confess, like Captain Ahab in *Moby Dick,* that all their methods are sane, their goal mad.

The perennial fascination of Greek philosophy lies in its concern with the kind of knowledge that led man out of his brutish existence. Science would be just an instrument for comfort and power, not a cultural force, if it did not help man to transcend his animal origin. Whatever their selfish interests and their commitments to practical ends, most scientists cling to the faith—respected in the spirit even though often betrayed in action—that to work for knowledge and truth is the highest form of scientific duty. Ideally, and to a large extent actually, science is part of the collective effort for the humanization of mankind.

Modern science has been immensely successful in discovering facts and inventing techniques. But only a few minds in each generation have been able to perceive the laws of the cosmos and to communicate them in a meaningful form to their less gifted fellow men. As to understanding the nature of the universe and of the human condition, it is questionable whether we have progressed much during the past two thousand years.

Let us look at the field of biology. It seems to me that the scientific attitude of modern biologists is conditioned to a very large extent by assumptions about the mind-matter problem which were made a few centuries ago and which are accepted as a basis of operation without concern for their validity, even by those who do not really believe in them.

During the early seventeenth century, as is well known, René Descartes asserted that the human body and the human soul are two separate entities and that the body is a machine which, therefore, can be studied as such. This was a convenient assumption and one which has proved extremely useful for certain kinds of scientific pursuits. Immediately following Descartes, scientists applied what they knew of mechanics to the body machine and found that its structure and functions were compatible with the knowledge derived from lifeless systems. Then the chemists and the physicists engaged in similar studies and found that the phenomena associated with life obey at each step the same physicochemical laws that operate in the inanimate world. At the present time this approach to the study of the structure and functions of living things is culminating in the marvelous achievements of molecular biology.

The fact that Descartes's assumptions have led to such great scientific advances does not prove, however, that these assumptions are correct. There is no evidence whatever that the body and the mind are two separate entities, and despite the triumphs of molecular biology, it has not yet been proven that the living body is only a machine and that life is merely a complex integration of known physicochemical forces. I realize that in raising this question I may seem to be reviving the vitalistic doctrine with all its false intellectual mysticism. But, in my opinion, I am doing nothing of the sort. I am only emphasizing that the machine view of living things is buried so deep in the modern subconscious that few scientists ever try to bring it to the surface to examine its significance in the bright light of critical knowledge. And I believe that the acceptance of an oversimplified mechanistic theory of life has narrowed considerably the front of progress in biological sciences.

Increasingly during recent decades the study of biological problems has been influenced by two large assumptions which at first sight appear to be based on hard-boiled scientific common sense, but in reality are still *sub judice*. One is that life can be understood only by analyzing the mechanisms linking the molecular and the animate worlds; the other is that the arrow of influence between these two worlds points in only one direction, from the molecular lifeless components to the more complex patterns of organization found in living things. These two assumptions have been immensely fruitful because they have encouraged investigators to break down phenomena and structures into smaller and simpler components, ultimately to be described in terms of identifiable chemical forces and substances. Moreover, they provide the easiest and safest approach to biology. They free the scientist from the need to engage in soul searching about the philosophical meaning of life, since in the final analysis they equate living processes with the reactions of inanimate matter. Finally, they permit an endless series of laboratory operations, because to disintegrate and analyze is far easier than to build up complex functioning organisms or even to investigate them as a whole. In the words of Professor Homer W. Smith:

> I would define mechanism, as we use the word today, as designating the belief that all the activities of the living organism are ultimately to be explained in terms of its component molecular parts. This was Descartes's greatest contribution to philosophy. . . . Abandon Cartesian mechanism and you will close up every scientific biological laboratory in the world at once, you will turn back the clock by three full centuries.

It is likely, however, that if the analytical breakdown of living things into simpler and ever simpler components is not supplemented by a more synthetic approach, it will lead the biologist into areas of knowledge concerned not with the essential characteristics of life but with a few selected phenomena which happen to be associated with living processes. To accept this limitation is an attitude of intellectual security and may be the better part of wisdom, but it denies scientists the chance to gain deeper insight into larger biological realities. As a contrast to the unphilosophical endless accretion of "scientific" facts concerning living *matter,* it is stimulating to rediscover in Aristotle's writing the entrancing throb of life. Darwin had this experience on reading William Ogle's translation of *The Parts of Animals.* "I had not the most remote notion what a wonderful man he was," wrote Darwin. "Linnaeus and Cuvier have been my two gods, though in very different ways, but they were mere schoolboys to old Aristotle."

It seems to me that a return to the Aristotelian philosophy, far from being a retreat, would enlarge the scope of the biological sciences. Biology will run dry unless it becomes more receptive than it is presently to unsuspected phenomena, unpredictable on the basis of what is already known. Science does not progress only by inductive, analytical knowledge. The imaginative speculations of the mind come first, the verification and the analytic breakdown come only later. And imagination depends upon a state of emotional and intellectual freedom which makes the mind receptive to the impressions that it receives from the world in its confusing, overpowering, but enriching totality. We must try to experience again the receptivity of the young ages of science when it was socially acceptable to marvel. What Baudelaire said of art applies equally well to science: "Genius is youth recaptured." More prosaically, I believe that in most cases the creative scientific act comes before the operations which lead to the establishment of truth; together they make science.

Nothing could illustrate better the change that occurred in the focus of the scientific community during the Industrial Revolution than the sudden and complete disappearance of the term "natural philosophy." The schism between science and philosophy was the result of two forces which operated almost simultaneously. One was the recognition that knowledge could be used for creating wealth and power; the other was the rapid accumulation of new and unexpected facts which engendered a sense of humility before the complexity of nature and rendered scientists shy of extrapolating from factual knowledge into speculative thoughts. Then humility evolved into scorn for speculation, and today the statement "This is not science, this is philosophy" rules out of scientific discussion any statement that goes a step beyond established fact.

Yet it is apparent that today, as in the past, many scientists—among them some of the most brilliant and most effective—are eager to escape from the austere discipline of factual knowledge and to experience again the intoxication of philosophical thought. They may distrust Plato, but, like him, they seem to regard philosophy as the "dear delight." Witness the flurry of speculative books published by scientists as soon as some discovery enlarges the scope of their knowledge. The theory of evolution has been used by biologists as a platform to erect or justify religious, political, and economic philosophies. Familiarity with modern theoretical physics seems to warrant opinions not only on the structure of matter and its relation to energy but also on the nature of life, the existence of free will, or the symbolism of language.

This return to scientific philosophy negates, it seems to me, the fears so commonly expressed that scientists are becoming a class apart from the rest of society by developing a culture without contact with the rest of human life. It is true, of course, that within the area of his particular work each scientist becomes so specialized that he finds it difficult to communicate on scientific subjects except with other workers in the same specialized field. But this situation is not peculiar to science. It exists just as much in other forms of learning—in philology or Moslem culture as much as in mathematics or genetics. Moreover, science should not be regarded as one single discipline concerning which sweeping statements can be made, any more than this can be done for the so-called humanities. With regard to the knowledge and operations defined by their techniques, the biologist and the mathematician are as far apart as they are from the student of Sanskrit or from the art critic, and as these are from each other. We must accept as a fact that the modern world is made up of an immense number of specialized groups, intellectually separated by experience, words, and the meaning of symbols. In my opinion, there are not "two cultures," even though C. P. Snow has made the expression famous. There are a multiplicity of intellectual occupations, each of which fortunately has several points of contact with human life. Whatever his field of specialization, the scholar can be understood beyond the confines of his guild—but only if he is willing to raise his language above the jargon of his trade. The scholar must learn to speak to man.

As we have seen, the transformations of human life which have taken place during the past hundred years are the realizations of the utopias formulated by the seventeenth- and eighteenth-century philosophers. Not so long ago the role of the scientist in this enterprise appeared straightforward and all to the good; each advance in scientific knowledge eventually resulted in some contributions to human health and happiness. Confident of the ultimate beneficence of his work, the scientist had good reasons to keep aloof from social problems. It is obvious, however, that the situation is now changing rapidly, and one can anticipate that the scientist will face more and more problems of conscience as the social power of science continues to increase.

The issues that immediately come to mind are certain obvious threats to mankind such as those associated with atomic power or with population pressures. In fact, however, the scientist's responsibility is involved in many other issues which appear less dramatic, perhaps, but are probably as important in the long run and more difficult to solve because less clearly defined. Until very recent times so little could be done to deal with the obvious shortages and sufferings in the world that the most urgent need was to develop techniques for the production of material wealth and for the control of disease. Now the power of science is so great that almost any desired method, gadget, or product can be developed if we are willing to devote enough resources to the task. And it is precisely the confidence that utopias can now be converted into realities which creates urgent ethical problems for the scientist.

The question of how to do things was a purely technical one that could be decided on scientific criteria; but the choice of *what* to do, among all the things that can be done, clearly implies some concern with ultimate social consequences. There is no longer any thoughtful person who believes that the conversion of science into more power, more wealth, or more drugs necessarily adds to health and happiness or improves the human condition. Indeed, haphazard scientific technology pursued without regard for its relevance to the meaning of human life could spell the end of civilization. Unless he becomes concerned with social philosophy, the scientist will increasingly hear the words of Oscar Wilde applied to him: that he knows the price of everything, but the value of nothing.

Equally distinguished as a bacteriologist and statesman of science, René Dubos is a member of the Rockefeller Institute for Medical Research. Among his books is a definitive biography of Louis Pasteur. This article is drawn from a series of lectures at Brookhaven National Laboratory, to be published as a book by the Columbia University Press.

At the tip of
CAPE COD

Salty Provincetown still harbors its fishing fleet, but the summertime visitor may feel a good deal closer to the Left Bank than the Grand Banks

By ROBERT HATCH

PHOTOGRAPHED FOR HORIZON BY ARNOLD NEWMAN

Edward Hopper (opposite) has been summering on Cape Cod for thirty years. He and his wife live in this studio-house in South Truro. Its big window looks toward Provincetown ten miles away. Hopper—a man who values his privacy—does not regret the distance. Though probably the best-known painter on the Cape, he stays aloof from its art colony. *Rooms by the Sea* (above), which is in the Stephen C. Clark Collection, is a view from his front door.

COURTESY PROVINCETOWN ART ASSOCIATION

This old photograph shows Charles W. Hawthorne, founder of the Provincetown art colony and for thirty years its most famous teacher, giving an open-air demonstration on how to paint the figure. Now there is not much figure painting going on there, and even less outdoors.

At the tip of Cape Cod, somewhere along the four-mile stretch between Race Point and Wood End, there once stood a colony of fishermen's shacks and hovels of illicit entertainment known as Helltown. It was swept away a century ago, and now along there it is all public beach, brightly spattered in season with umbrellas, singing with the cries of children and portable radios, and patrolled by that insanely patient breed, the surf caster. But there are those who will tell you, between sorrow and anger, that the name of that scandalous old appendage to Provincetown should be revived and applied anew to the whole town. Certainly no one coming upon the place for the first time on one of those glassy days of July or August will suppose he has stumbled on Paradise.

Thrust twenty-five miles out into the Atlantic and curving for three miles around one of the East Coast's most beautiful harbors, Provincetown can seem an evil-smelling, brazen-throated honky-tonk. There it squats at the end of sixty-five miles of superhighway, its approach an appalling clutter of cabins, motels, and ice-cream stands (which, however, belong to Truro and keep that peaceful town in tax money). The road was built to carry the vacation caravans of Boston, Worcester, Providence, New York, Philadelphia, Washington, and the eastern provinces of Canada; and Provincetown waits at the end with two narrow, parallel streets that produce a traffic snarl raised to the pitch of burlesque. This is the town where even the pedestrians jam up. Men have been seen fleeing Provincetown with the fixed grin of apocalypse on their faces—indeed, they may be seen so fleeing any day in summer, and they make the Cape-Enders chuckle.

Provincetown has always been an embarrassment to the rest of Cape Cod. As early as 1727 Truro petitioned to be separated from its uncouth neighbor, and it is the regular practice of residents of Dennis, Harwich, and the other staider communities up-Cape to volunteer the assurance that they never go near the dreadful place. They resent it and mistrust it the way the country at large resents and mistrusts New York. Provincetown is a metropolis carved on the head of a pin.

Like a big city, it has its roots in history. It was here that the Pilgrims first landed, befriended the Indians and robbed them, and wrote the Mayflower Compact. The great tower, which is the first thing you see of Provincetown by sea, by land, or by air, commemorates the month-long sojourn of the Pilgrims in that crescent harbor. It is a much grander monument than the Rock with which, according to Cape Codders, Plymouth has tried to usurp glory, and it has the touch of crazy incongruity that makes it appropriate for Provincetown: it is a slightly inaccurate copy of the Torre del Mangia in Siena, a place not otherwise closely associated with Governor William Bradford and his company.

Provincetown is the only community on Cape Cod today with a major industry other than tourists. It is one of the important fishing ports of the Atlantic, and that keeps it in daily touch with the Boston and New York markets and lends it a worldliness quite unlike the localized preoccupations of other small towns. And like a big city, Provincetown's population is a mingling of strains. The original New England stock, which styled the architecture, named the streets, and built the whaling fleets and the Banks schooners, is still there but is overshadowed today by the Portuguese, mainly from the Azores, who now man the fishing boats and to a large extent control the affairs of the town. The Portuguese are probably more tolerant of the oddities of Bohemians and summer boarders than the original natives would have been. They are devout Catholics and conservative in their traditions, but they are Latins and have themselves come a long way from home. The atmosphere of the town might be called congenial but volatile, with flare-ups to be anticipated in August. A night or two in jail has never been taken much to heart in Provincetown; it is only when proceedings must be moved to the county seat at Barnstable that people shake their heads.

Finally, Provincetown has a cultural life entirely disproportionate to its size. It would be inaccurate to call this a local culture, for it is sustained largely by people who live there only in the summer; nevertheless it is based solidly in the history and institutions of the town, and it extends unbroken back at least to the beginning of the century. Provincetown has never been an artists' colony in the sense that Rockport or Woodstock are artists' colonies. It is a town with a life of its own that also attracts writers and painters. If there were room for one on this spit of sand, Provincetown might have a Left Bank. As it is, the various communities—the two-week vacationists, the semi-retired psychoanalysts, the artists and writers, the fishermen, and the old ladies in bonnets (who are largely invisible from the Fourth of July to Labor Day) live swirled together as though dropped there by a particularly high tide.

Painting is the senior art of Provincetown and the one that dominates its cultural life today. Charles W. Hawthorne established his famous school there in 1899, and ever since, easels and buoys have been the twin symbols of the town. But the writers were the ones who first gave Provincetown its popular fame—and specifically it was Eugene O'Neill. In the years during and just after World War I, George Cram Cook, Susan Glaspell, Hutchins Hapgood, Sinclair Lewis, John Reed, Wilbur Daniel Steele, and Mary Heaton Vorse were all living there. So also was Robert Edmond Jones, the stage designer. With such a group, a theater was almost inevitable, and in the summer of 1915 a large fishhouse standing on a wharf was cleared of its stored dories and nets and fitted with a stage and benches (sliding doors could be opened behind the stage to turn the harbor into a set). One of the plays put on that first season, *Suppressed Desires* by Cook and Susan Glaspell, has become a standard work in the country's little-theater repertory.

The next summer O'Neill was in town, and one evening he brought the theater group his *Bound East for Cardiff* for a trial reading. One after another the early sea plays of O'Neill were performed on the old wharf, and the Provincetown Players were on their way to becoming the most brilliant company in America. They reached their peak, however, not on the Cape but in New York—the great years of the Provincetown Players were on MacDougal Street.

After the war the writers began to drift apart—John Reed went to Moscow and wrote *Ten Days that Shook the World;* George Cram Cook died in Athens. Writers continued to live in Provincetown: John Dos Passos was there for many years, and only last summer Norman Mailer was seized by the police for yelling "Taxi!" in ironic appreciation of one of their resplendent prowl cars. But for a generation now it has been a painter's town.

Schools have given Provincetown its continuity as an art center. Hawthorne's was one of the most important in the country until his death in 1930; four years later Hans Hofmann arrived in town, a refugee from the Nazis, to found a school which, both in Provincetown and during the winter in New York, has been a major stimulus of the abstract expressionism that now makes American painting a leading force in Western art. This season about a dozen schools are in session—from the Cape School, which Henry Hensche, once Hawthorne's assistant, has run for thirty years according to the principles of his old master, to the Provincetown Workshop, a school that has been booming for the past few summers under the direction of Victor Candell and Leo Manso. It encourages large canvases, and can do so because

Even at low tide on a sunless July day, Provincetown's harbor is one of the most picturesque in the East. The tall Italianate tower commemorates,

it operates on two floors of an abandoned public school.

The battle between tradition and experiment has been fought through the studios of Provincetown almost from the beginning. Until recently the Provincetown Art Association applied the wisdom of Solomon to the problem: it cut the colony in two and let the modernists have a show in July, with the traditionalists making a rebuttal in August. The Art Association was formed in 1914 by a group of painters who, with singular wisdom, elected William H. Young, the town's leading banker, to the presidency. Mr. Young served until 1937, with the result that the mortgages and building loans of the steadily growing organization never outstripped its resources. The Association continues to have two jury shows a summer; they are no longer segregated, and season by season abstraction gains over tradition. Each summer, also, the letter columns of the Provincetown *Advocate* are enlivened by the controversy between those who think the Association juries are too easygoing in their admission standards and those who threaten perpetual boycott because a work of theirs has been rejected.

Provincetown and its surrounding dunes, bays, and highlands have almost ceased to serve painters as subject matter. Artists gravitate there because of the tradition, because of the community, and because like everyone else they like sun and salt water. And they come to sell their work. Studios and schools and art associations are the common institutions of towns where artists congregate; but the commercial galleries are something new in Provincetown and something unmatched elsewhere (we are not talking of New York, London, or Paris). Of course, paintings have always been sold in

rather oddly, the Pilgrim Fathers; more in the New England vein is the fine old church to the left of it, now become the Chrysler Art Museum

Provincetown—artists did business from their studios, the Art Association took a commission on work sold, and various short-lived ventures were attempted by part-time, semiprofessional dealers. But, by and large, the work that sold over the counter was in the souvenir category—a nice boat with sea gulls or Highland Light by moonlight.

Now there are eight or more commercial galleries in town, and not infrequently they sell paintings for sums that only a maharajah would offer for a souvenir. They hang carefully designed one-man and group shows, hold formal openings (some as often as every ten days), and draw patronage from the art-buying public of the whole country. People now make the rounds of the Provincetown galleries the way they used to make the rounds on Fifty-seventh Street before New York City's art center was dispersed. It is fun if you enjoy looking at paintings, for work of quality and often of excellence—traditional, experimental, and abstract—can be seen both day and night along the three-mile stretch of Commercial Street. And it is exciting if you are a collector-speculator, for mixed in with established names and price tags sometimes as high as four figures, is work by unknown painters that has been chosen for showing by a group of canny and competitive dealers. Reputations are flown like kites in Provincetown, and people who fancy backing what pleases them find that money burns their fingers.

The market fever is undoubtedly affecting the painters. They used to come to Provincetown to work and teach and argue; now they must be uncommonly pure or uncommonly successful to ignore the bustling exchange. Everyone is aware of how the galleries are doing from one weekend to the next (is a spell of rain bad because it keeps people off the Cape or good because it drives them in from the beaches?), and a lot of politics goes into the business of getting hung in the shops with the best locations or the most resourceful managements.

All this is heightened, particularly among the younger artists, by the presence of Walter P. Chrysler, Jr., who bought a place near Provincetown a few years ago and who in 1958 brought a considerable portion of his collection to town and opened the Chrysler Art Museum in what had been the Central Methodist Church. The building had become unsafe and the congregation lacked funds to repair it, so Chrysler saved for the town one of its largest and most beautiful landmarks—though he also jazzed it up a bit with fancy landscaping and floodlights.

Chrysler is a patron, but a somewhat mysterious one. He likes to play hunches and he likes to drive bargains. He is thus a subject of constant rumor. The story will sweep town that he has bought *fifty* canvases from someone hitherto only narrowly renowned; it will be reported on good authority that so-and-so, not previously considered a very interesting performer, is about to be hung in the Museum, and his stock will zoom, the very word "museum" having a golden sound.

All of this makes art an uneasy profession in Provincetown and is one factor that makes the future more than usually hazy. Another factor is the rising cost of living; Provincetown is no longer cheap. It becomes increasingly difficult to find a shack, to say nothing of a studio; and if the town has its way, large sections of the Province Lands, that great sweep of state-owned wilderness back toward the ocean, where squatters were always tolerated, will be developed for vacationists. Fishing is not what it once was, and Provincetown may turn increasingly to trippers for its livelihood.

What keeps painters in the town is tradition, conviviality, the dunes, and the sea. Perhaps the galleries will also hold them, or perhaps they will find that they are happier shipping to market from some less clamorous haven. Plays—often O'Neill—are still produced out on a wharf. Jo Hawthorne, the son of Charles W., conducts the Provincetown Symphony in two admirable concerts a summer (the Cape also lures musicians), and smaller groups perform almost every week. Behind the honky-tonk store fronts and up the alleys too narrow for the traffic to escape into, the life of Provincetown is still rich. The artists have weathered wars and depressions out on their land's end. It remains to be seen if they will weather the prosperity of a four-lane highway, regular plane schedules to Boston, rich patrons, a hectic art market, and a real-estate boom. The harbor does not change—except as it changes with every shift of light and wind and tide. It would not be easy to leave.

Robert Hatch has been a summertime Cape-Ender ever since war years. He is the literary editor of The Nation *and its regular film critic, as well as the theater critic of* HORIZON.

Hans Hofmann (opposite) took up in Provincetown where Charles W. Hawthorne left off. "It was my destiny," he says, "to fill the vacuum." He arrived there in the summer of 1934, four years after Hawthorne's death, and started a school that in its time has been as important as his predecessor's was. Hofmann's influence has been immense. As a much-loved teacher who has shaped a whole generation of American artists and as an innovating painter in his own right, he has been, as much as anyone, a leader of the abstract expressionist movement that has dominated American art for about fifteen years. In 1958 he gave up teaching to paint full time. He is now eighty-one, but confidently points out that Titian was still painting at ninety-nine. Behind him is a work in progress, *String Quartet,* to which he has pinned pieces of colored paper as a way of testing what he plans to do next. He owns an old house on Commercial Street. Its exterior is primly Colonial—white with black shutters—but inside Mrs. Hofmann has painted the walls gleaming white and the floors and furniture in vigorous shades of blue, yellow, green, and tomato red.

Franz Kline (left) says he likes Provincetown because it is "both quiet and jazzy," qualities that are not always so impartially admired by other residents. Kline insures his quiet by living on a back street and keeping his telephone number unlisted; but as an artist in the very front rank of the abstract expressionists, he is hardly an anonymous figure, and knowing tourists have no trouble spotting him as he drives around town in his Jaguar. Behind his rambling Colonial house is a large boat-builder's barn that he has converted into a studio. Here he has ample room to paint the huge, slashing canvases for which he is internationally famous. For some years these were austerely black and white, but Kline continues the investigation of color begun with his former teacher Henry Hensche, and not long ago he reintroduced color into his own paintings with brilliant effect.

Karl Knaths (opposite) has been going to Provincetown for more than forty years, and for the past ten has lived there year-round in a house that he and his wife built in 1923. It is in the West End, almost at the tip of the Cape, set well back from Commercial Street. Knaths's skylighted studio is on the second floor, and here—after a walk on the dunes or along the waterfront—he spends his mornings painting the unmistakable expressionist canvases that have earned him a place in the major American museums (the one he has been working on here is called *Captain and Crew*). He achieves his masterly orchestration of color by carefully planning the chromatic range of a painting in advance, as a composer might select his keys. Once the scheme is set, he never departs from it. The colors are mixed in clamshells and kept together in the drawer of a bureau until the painting is finished.

DITTO

Leo Manso and ***Victor Candell*** conduct the largest and probably the liveliest art school among the dozen or so that are in session on the Cape every summer. Called the Provincetown Workshop, it occupies two spacious rooms (this is one of them) on the second floor of a former school building. In the photograph, each man is seated before one of his own paintings—Manso at the left with *Soldia*, a title he invented for one of a series of sun paintings, and Candell at the right with *Midnight Growth*. The other canvases are all the work of their students, of whom they have about forty, almost evenly divided between earnest young tyros and adults who have had some previous training. Because the youngsters are usu-

ally poor and life in Provincetown is by no means cheap, the two men have started a scholarship plan that will hopefully accommodate ten students a season. This is only the Workshop's third summer, but Manso and Candell are trying to build it into an important school that teaches good painting without promoting any "official" style. Already the atmosphere is serious and stimulating; and if most of the work is abstract, that is because it seems a perfectly natural idiom to the young—but the two proprietors are not doctrinaire about it. The other schools in Provincetown are smaller and more single-minded in approach, but together they cover the whole range from avant-garde to the most conservative.

Jack Tworkov (opposite) first went to Provincetown as a student in the early twenties and has been going back, off and on, ever since. Three years ago he bought his own house—age uncertain—and added this studio at the back. It is big enough to enable him to work on three canvases at once, and Tworkov is no miniaturist: one of the paintings in his last show measured eight feet by six and a half. Of the three seen here, only *Boon* at the left is near completion; the other two, *Thursday* and *Brake II,* are not as far along. His style is vigorously abstract expressionist, and no one should look for any literal connection between his paintings and the Cape Cod landscape—but he says he finds inspiration in it, especially in the color and texture of the marshes around Wellfleet in the autumn.

Sol Wilson (below) and his wife spend their summers in a small house tucked in beside the water at the east end of Commercial Street. The view of the harbor is one of the best in Provincetown, although it has been made considerably less picturesque by a storm that swept away the ruined wharf in the background, and thereby deprived Wilson of an especially congenial subject. He used to teach, but gave it up several years ago to devote all of his time to painting landscapes and cityscapes (he lives in New York in the winter). During the summer he travels up and down the Cape looking for subject matter, making quick pen-and-ink sketches from which he works up his paintings later in his attic studio. The finished canvas on the easel is a characteristic down-Cape scene called *Low Tide.*

The Provincetown Art Association was founded in 1914 to stimulate interest in art. It is true that its stimuli frequently produce abrupt and violent reactions—hardly a summer passes that some dissident artist does not publicly accuse it of perfidy or stupidity—but it is also true that the Association is in large measure responsible for the continuity and stability of Provincetown's reputation as an art center. Shown here is a representative group of members, photographed in the Association's handsome new wing with examples of their work. As keyed at the left, the artists and

their respective paintings are: (1) Umberto Romano, who recently moved his summer art school from Gloucester to Provincetown, and *African Image;* (2) Seong Moy, an eminent print maker and painter, and *The Stolen Kiss;* (3) George Yater, the Association's longtime director, and *Trap Boat at Dawn;* (4) Henry Hensche, a devoted pupil of Charles Hawthorne, and *Sunlight*; (5) Byron Browne, who every summer paints a portrait of a fellow artist but is represented here by *Night Sail;* (6) Morris Davidson and his abstract *Black on Ochre;* (7) Ross Moffett, one of the earliest members of the Association, and *Provincetown Historical Museum;* (8) Irving Marantz and *Yellow Cloud over Race Point;* (9) Henry Botkin and *Transition No. 2;* (10) Joe Kaplan and his subdued, moody *Dune;* (11) Peter Busa, one of the Association's early abstractionists, and *Oil Anchors;* (12) Bruce McKain, assistant director of the Association, and *Shore Line;* (13) Lily Harmon and a collage, *Enclosure*; (14) Gerrit Hondius and his *Still Life with Flowers;* (15) Harry Engel and *Acropolis Maiden;* and (16) Ben Wolf with his *Aunt Mary's Pond, Wellfleet.*

Chaim Gross (below) is a sculptor who produces the bulk of his happy, exuberant, and almost instantly appealing work (the cunningly balanced *Young Acrobats* shown here is typical) during the winter months in New York. In Provincetown, to which he has been coming regularly ever since 1943, sculpture is an occupation for rainy days; he prefers to spend the bright summer mornings at drawing and painting. Gross riding a bicycle and wearing an embroidered *yarmelka* used to be one of the town's most engaging and familiar sights. He still wears the cap, but now rides in an old yellow Cadillac.

Boris Margo and his wife ***Jan Gelb*** (right) live in enviable isolation on the dunes: their shack is built almost exactly on the site of the old Coast Guard station once inhabited by Eugene O'Neill (that building long ago succumbed to the sea). They have no telephone, no electricity, and no road—but their front yard is a magnificent sweep of sea and sand. Margo also has a studio hidden away in town where he works and teaches a few advanced students. Miss Gelb paints at home. She is shown holding her *Sunset Chord,* while Margo leans on his characteristically muted *Pulsation of Oneness.*

Milton Avery (below) ranged widely—from the Gaspé Peninsula to Mexico and Europe—before he began summering in Provincetown four years ago. Wherever he is, he paints; and his recent work includes many views of the harbor and of the down-Cape landscape, such as the *Dunes and Sea* that forms a background for this portrait. Avery's painting has never been wholly abstract, but the subject matter is always simplified and heightened to impart his own particular and poetic vision. His use of color and distortion and thinly applied paint may remind one of Matisse, but the style remains distinctively and stubbornly American. His close and happy family ties have often been reflected in his work, which includes many paintings of his wife, Sally Michel, an illustrator, and of his daughter March, now married. He once held a one-man show called "My Daughter, March."

Edwin Dickinson (opposite) is a major American artist whose work is not widely known to the public, even though he has been painting steadily and masterfully for almost fifty years. He is one of the few members of the National Academy of Design to be given a respectful showing at the Museum of Modern Art, and that may be a clue: his art does not fit any of the easy categories. It is modern but grounded in tradition, representational but not realistic, and its subject matter, though always identifiable, is somehow mysterious. The success of a big retrospective show last winter in New York, his first there since 1943, may be a sign that the public is at last beginning to value his work on its own terms. Dickinson first went to Provincetown in 1912 to study with Hawthorne and has maintained close ties there ever since, although he now lives in Wellfleet.

By WILLIAM HARLAN HALE

A MEMORANDUM

From: Ex-Secretary of State Thomas Jefferson

To: Secretary of State Dean Rusk

Subject: On enlarging our house of diplomacy

Sensible of the multitudinous public burdens you bear, I hesitate to afflict you with correspondence from one in retirement and without claim on your indulgence. And if I intrude upon you as a sometime holder of the office you now grace, it is with a lively sense of the chasm that separates our conditions and occasions. How small were mine, when I ponder the immensity of yours!

Indeed, such were the limitations of my day and station that when I first organized a Department of State at the behest of General Washington, a small dwelling-house hard by the President's own on High Street in Philadelphia more than sufficed for it; for my establishment consisted of just five clerks, two messengers, and a French interpreter, while our envoys abroad then also numbered five. But you, I understand, are presently assisted at Washington by nearly seven thousand souls (a fraction of your total diplomatic establishment of about twenty-three thousand), who are housed in a newly completed edifice greater by far than any other chancellery in the world. I humble myself before the magnitude of your undertakings, and trust that they are dictated by necessity. You would not, sir, I am certain, as a fellow devotee of that Party which I once sought to dedicate to the cause of wise and frugal government, admit any superfluities in office. It may even be that greater numbers in diplomacy, when necessary, have the virtue of infusing democracy into that hitherto all too aristocratic art.

I shrink, however, from contemplation of the State Department's new edifice itself, for which, I know, you are not yourself responsible, having received it as part of your legacy from the previous administration of the opposite party. I ask myself whether you may not also have inherited an incubus. I presume it is a law of progress that governments must grow. As they grow, they require larger buildings. As they build larger buildings, governments in turn must grow to fill them. The other party has now built quite the biggest building ever known to diplomacy, and upon you devolves the task of keeping it filled and bustling, lest you be charged with dereliction and sloth.

Yet what a blank, forbidding pile it is for the opposition to have erected in the name of our foreign affairs in the city of my high hopes! It must be seen before your problems can be believed. A half-mile of faceless façades; mazes of interior passageways; seven cavernous stories of cubicles and suites, tier on tier; six separate entries to add confusion to the lower depths; and a general atmosphere of a subterranean rabbit warren of nameless officialdom: Is not all this, sir, in addition to being repellent to the aesthetic senses, an effort by the opposition to obstruct and frustrate your own efforts to bring light and grace to bear upon our matters of state? The military, in whom we cannot always assume good taste, constructed their monstrous Pentagon, and have been at odds with each other ever since; you now have fallen heir to a civilian Pentagon with protocol, but without half so original a shape.

Casting my eye over the rise of our Republic—and we are all Republicans when we are not also Democrats—I ask myself why it is that the larger our diplomatic occasions have grown, the worse our architecture for housing them has be-

DRAWING BY ANTHONY SARIS

come. Is it because at heart we dislike our foreign engagements and in this manner show our fundamental hostility to them? In my day, although I eschewed entangling alliances, my little brick State Department house in Philadelphia was at least hospitable in appearance. It was followed at the new capital by a succession of offices of increasing size and decreasing style as America advanced toward world stature. The government abandoned my simplicities in favor of the grand façade and finally of the powerhouse. Yet I shall breathe no word here against "Old State," that mansarded oddity of the time of President Grant, which was the last of your buildings to have at least some style.

"Old State," the greatest Federal pile then built, served your Department through several wars and crises with its gimcrack porticoes and the calm of its potted aspidistras and slowly turning fans. Yet you abandoned it (under a Democratic President, I regret to say) a little less than fifteen years ago to move on to "New State," that vast antiseptic barracks built originally for the military in the city's swampland still appropriately known, I believe, as Foggy Bottom. Now you have abandoned *that* to move on to the still newer warren adjoining it, three times larger than the last, and which I presume you call "*New*, New State."

It was, I understand, designed to be an "annex." Annex indeed! Never has an outgrowth so overwhelmed its parent. Threefold expansion in half a generation! I shudder to think what the next few years may bring. Will you enclose all Northern Virginia in glass as headquarters of the free world?

In my primeval time, a diplomatic visitor was led directly into my own office. Even later, in "Old State," one outer reception room sufficed for the privacy of the Secretary. Then, in "New State"—or, we had best now say "Old New State"—our affairs having multiplied, a suite of rooms around an interior corridor was constructed for him. But in your "New, New State," I observe, the inner secretarial suite has taken on the length of a city block—so great have we become. Indeed, sir, few monarchs of the past have required passage through so many antechambers to enter the sovereign presence as the Secretary of State does now into his; and not even the immense flights of the late tyrant Hitler in the Wilhelmstrasse or of his colleague Mussolini in the Palazzo Venezia were more oppressive, architecturally, than these. Meanwhile your President himself, I observe, still adheres to the gracious Executive Mansion of my own era. Does this possibly signify that it is just in our foreign affairs that America has become byzantine and impenetrable?

I can only hope that you, who have unwittingly inherited this cavern, will not of necessity be imprisoned by it. As you sit at the seventh-floor summit of your concrete pyramid composed of the hives of your undersecretaries, deputy undersecretaries, assistant secretaries, deputy assistant secretaries, and *their* caves of counselors, advisers, co-ordinators, bureau chiefs, area subchiefs, desk sub-subchiefs, administrative assistants, and *their* assistants, pray do not despair. At least your empire has windows, which still can be opened despite the air conditioning. So I trust you may succeed despite your surroundings, and that the prudence of our Republic will yet survive its architects.

The richly painted caverns at Lascaux in southwestern France were a gathering place for paleolithic man some twenty thousand years ago. Relatively small and never inhabited, they were used by many generations of hunting peoples for ceremonial ritual. What was important in these rites was not so much the finished painting itself as the act of painting: the walls of the caves are crowded with vivid images of oxen, horses, and deer, painted one over the other.

DIRECTORATE-GENERAL OF ANTIQUITIES, IRAQ

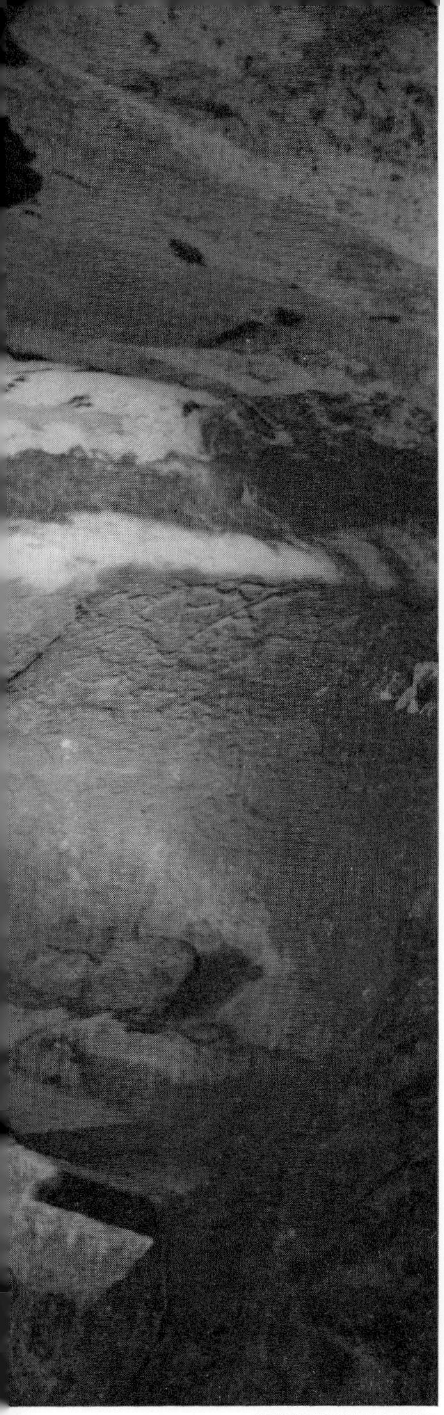

ARCHIVES PHOTOGRAPHIQUE

Six layers down beneath an eroded Sumerian temple in Iraq, adults and children of the prehistoric city of Eridu lie in rows in the town's cemetery of some one thousand graves.

CEMETERY AND CAVE

Amid the uneasy wanderings of paleolithic man, the dead were the first to have a permanent dwelling: a cavern, a mound marked by a cairn, a collective barrow. These were landmarks to which the living probably returned at intervals, to commune with or placate the ancestral spirits. Though food-gathering and hunting do not encourage the permanent occupation of a single site, the dead at least claim that privilege. Long ago, the Jews claimed as their patrimony the land where the graves of their forefathers were situated; and that well-attested claim seems a primordial one. The city of the dead antedates the city of the living.

There is another part of the environment that paleolithic man not merely used but periodically came back to: the cave. There is plenty of evidence, all over the world, of the aboriginal occupation or visitation of caves. In the limestone caves of the Dordogne in France, for instance, early man's successive occupations can be traced in layers, as the erosion of the rock lowered the river bed, raising old shelters and exposing new platforms lower down. But more important than its use for domestic purposes was the part that the cave played in art and ritual.

In the inner recesses of such special ritual centers, usually reached by low passages, demanding a tortuous and frequently dangerous crawl, one finds great natural chambers, covered with paintings of astonishing vividness of form and facility of design, chiefly of exquisitely realistic animals, occasionally of highly formalized and stylized men and women.

In going back so far for the origins of the city, one must not of course overlook the practical needs that drew family groups and tribes together seasonally in a common habitat, a series of camp sites, even in a collecting or a hunting economy. These played their parts, too; and long before agricultural villages and towns became a feature of the neolithic culture, the favorable sites for them had probably been prospected: the pure spring with its year-round supply of water, the solid hummock of land, accessible, yet protected by river or swamp, the nearby estuary heavily stocked with fish and shellfish—all these served already in many regions for the intermediary mesolithic economy, on sites whose permanence is witnessed by huge mounds of opened shells.

But note that two of the three original aspects of temporary settlement have to do with sacred things, not just with physical survival: they relate to a more valuable and meaningful kind of life, with a consciousness that entertains past and future, apprehending the primal mystery of sexual generation and the ultimate mystery of death and what may lie beyond death. As the city takes form, much more will be added: but these central concerns abide as the very reason for the city's existence, inseparable from the economic substance that makes it possible. In the earliest gathering about a grave or a painted symbol, a great stone or a sacred grove, one has the beginning of a succession of civic institutions that range from the temple to the astronomical observatory, from the theater to the university.

AIR MINISTRY, CROWN COPYRIGHT RESERVED; OPPOSITE: ARLETTE MELLAART

Invisible on the ground but clearly seen from the air is the whole plan of a neolithic village as it existed some five thousand years ago. Varying shades of vegetation outline the drainage pattern established originally by the furrows and palisades of the now buried village. The photograph above, taken over the Foggia Plain in Italy, shows a round enclosure 240 yards across, containing fourteen smaller circles, each of which was a compound for the livestock and living quarters of a neolithic family. To its right is the outline of a smaller, apparently older, settlement. Life in these compounds was much the same as life today in some remote corners of the world, such as the great marshes in southern Iraq. A family of these marsh dwellers is seen at right in their hut made of reeds. Their village, Kirsuwa, consists of seven such huts; their primitive economy is based precariously on rice, fish, and the domestication of the water buffalo.

GAVIN MAXWELL

THE NEOLITHIC VILLAGE

Perhaps fifteen thousand years ago the archaeologist begins to find definite traces of permanent settlements, from India to the Baltic area: a culture based on the use of shellfish and fish, possibly seaweed, and planted tubers, doubtless supplemented by other less certain supplies of food.

Let me emphasize neolithic man's concentration on organic life and growth: not merely a sampling and testing of what nature had provided, but a discriminating selection and propagation, to such good purpose that historic man has not added a plant or animal of major importance to those domesticated or cultivated by neolithic communities. Domestication in all its aspects implies two large changes: permanence and continuity in residence, and the exercise of control and foresight over processes once subject to the caprices of nature. With this go habits of gentling and nurturing and breeding. Here woman's needs, woman's solicitudes, woman's intimacy with the processes of growth, woman's capacity for tenderness and love, must have played a dominating part. With the great enlargement of the food supply that resulted from the cumulative domestication of plants and animals, woman's central place in the new economy was established.

Woman's presence made itself felt in every part of the village: not least in its physical structures, with their protective enclosures, whose further symbolic meanings psychoanalysis has now tardily brought to light. Security, receptivity, enclosure, nurture—these functions belong to woman; and they take structural expression in every part of the village, in the house and the oven, the byre and the bin, the cistern, the storage pit, the granary, and from there pass on to the city, in the wall and the moat, and all inner spaces, from the atrium to the cloister. House and village, eventually the town itself, are woman writ large. If this seems a wild psychoanalytic conjecture, the ancient Egyptians stand ready to vouch for the identification. In Egyptian hieroglyphics, "house" or "town" may stand as symbols for "mother," as if to confirm the similarity of the individual and the collective nurturing function. In line with this, the more primitive structures—houses, rooms, tombs—are usually round ones: like the original bowl described in Greek myth, which was modeled on Aphrodite's breast.

Let us look more closely at the early village, as one must picture it in Mesopotamia and the Valley of the Nile between, say, 9,000 and 4,000 B.C. A heap of mud huts, baked, or of mud-and-reed construction, cramped in size, at first little better than a beaver's lodge. Everywhere, the village is a small cluster of families, from half a dozen to three score perhaps, each with its own hearth, its own household god, its own shrine, its own burial plot, within the house or in some common burial ground.

The embryonic structure of the city already existed in the village. House, shrine, cistern, public way, agora—not yet a specialized market—all first took form in the village: inventions and organic differentiations waiting to be carried further in the more complex structure of the city. What holds for the general structure of the village also holds for its institutions. The beginnings of organized morality, government, law, and justice existed in the Council of Elders of the neolithic village.

The clay figure above, unearthed last year in Turkey, is a neolithic fertility symbol. Writes Mumford: "If one had any doubt about woman's commanding original part, one could get confirmation from the earliest religious myths; for in them her dominating femininity also manifests extremely savage attributes that suggest she had taken over far too much of the masculine role. These attributes linger today in the terrible figure of the Hindu goddess, Kali. Certainly the most ancient Mesopotamian deity was Tiamat, the primeval mother of waters, as hostile to her rebellious sons as the classic Freudian patriarch; while the cult of Kybele, the Great Mother, as lover and fierce mistress, commanding lions, lingered far into historic times in Asia Minor, though she was supplemented by more gentle, maternal images, such as Demeter, Mother of Harvests."

MUSEUM OF FINE ARTS, BOSTON

THE ROLE OF KINGS

The final outbreak of inventions that attended the birth of the city probably happened within a few centuries. As far as the present record stands, grain cultivation, the plow, the potter's wheel, the sailboat, the draw loom, copper metallurgy, abstract mathematics, exact astronomical observation, the calendar, writing and other modes of intelligible discourse in permanent form, all came into existence at roughly the same time, around 3,000 B.C. give or take a few centuries. This constituted a technological expansion of human power whose only parallel is the change that has taken place in our own time.

What made this concentration and mobilization of power possible? What gave it the special form it took in the city, with a central religious and political nucleus, the citadel, dominating the entire social structure? What I am going to suggest as the key development here had already been presaged, at a much earlier stage, by the apparent evolution of the protective hunter into the tribute-gathering chief. Suddenly this figure assumed superhuman proportions: all his powers and prerogatives became immensely magnified, while those of his subjects, who no longer had a will of their own or could claim any life apart from that of the ruler, were correspondingly diminished.

What I would suggest is that the most important agent in effecting the change from a decentralized village economy to a highly organized urban economy, was the king, or rather, the institution of kingship. I suggest that one of the attributes of the ancient Egyptian god Ptah, as revealed in a document derived from the third millennium B.C.—*that he founded cities*—is the special and all but universal function of kings. In the urban implosion, the king stands at the center: he is the polar magnet that draws to the heart of the city and brings under the control of the palace and temple all the new forces of civilization.

Religion may well have played an essential role. Without the help of the rising priestly caste, the hunting chieftain could never have achieved the enlarged powers and cosmic authority that attended his elevation to kingship and widened his sphere of control. Both sacred power and temporal power became swollen by absorbing the new inventions of civilization; and the very need for an intelligent control of every part of the environment gave additional authority to those dedicated either to intelligence or control, the priest or monarch, often united in a single office.

Certainly by the time the archaeologist's spade unearths a recognizable city, he finds a walled precinct, a citadel, made of durable materials, even if the rest of the town lacks a wall or permanent structures. This holds from Uruk to Harappa. Within that precinct he usually finds three huge stone or baked-brick buildings, buildings whose very magnitude sets them aside from the other structures in the city: the palace, the granary, and the temple. The citadel itself has many marks of a sacred enclosure: the exaggerated height and thickness of these walls in the earliest cities—seventy-five feet thick at Khorsabad in Assyria—is significantly out of all proportion to the military means that then existed for assaulting them. It is only for their gods that men exert themselves so extravagantly. But what first was designed to ensure the god's favor may later have paid off in practice as more effective military protection. The symbolic purpose probably antedated the military function.

With kingship came war. Its original purpose was not, perhaps, foreign conquest but propitiation of the gods. In times of crisis when the gods appeared angry, nothing less than human sacrifice seemed called for; and the greatest sacrifice, in some primitive societies, was the king himself. When the city came into existence, this ritual was broadened: the king understandably began to seek sacrificial victims abroad, and instead of single victims, whole communities were slaughtered. The Assyrian King Ashurnasirpal, often represented in his priestly role (as in the amber statuette opposite), waged war constantly and conquered lands as far west as the Mediterranean. In the famous Sumerian "Stele of the Vultures" (a detail of which is shown above) King Eannatum of the city of Lagash strides at the head of his men, the bodies of his foe already ground underfoot and the prey of vultures. The monumental walls of a citadel, as seen below in a view of the Mesopotamian city of Mari, were a constant reminder of the awful power of the king: the complex of buildings at right is the palace, which covered eight and a half acres and in its time was considered one of the wonders of the world. War was thoroughly ingrained in the very nature of the early city, and no matter how nobly the city has served mankind, it has also served, throughout its history, as the seedbed of organized aggression and violence.

HILLPRECHT COLLECTION, FRIEDRICH SCHILLER UNIVERSITY, JENA; OPPOSITE: LOUVRE

The remarkable tablet above, made about 1,500 B.C., *presents the earliest city plan so far unearthed. Here is the whole Mesopotamian temple city of Nippur, with its main canal (double lines) dividing the city from top to bottom, the Euphrates River on the far left, and the most renowned of its temple precincts at the far right. A view of the priests' quarters of Nippur, as they look today, is shown at right. Nippur was dedicated to deities who had evolved considerably beyond the nature gods of early man. As the matriarchal society of neolithic times gave way to the city, male gods came to dominate the pantheon. The typical female deity was no longer the Earth Mother but the love goddess, Astarte, shown opposite above in a gold relief. Astarte incorporated all the more sophisticated aspects of her sexuality—tenderness, beauty, erotic delight: she was later to be fused with Aphrodite, Diana, and Juno.*

THE EARLIEST CITIES

The city represented a new degree of human concentration, a new magnitude in settlement. The ancient city of Ur, the early home of Abraham, with its canals, harbors, and temples, occupied 220 acres, while the walls of Uruk encompassed an area of just over two square miles. Khorsabad, about 700 B.C., enclosed some 740 acres; Nineveh, a century later, perhaps 1,800 acres; while later still, Babylon, before its destruction by the Persians, was surrounded by at least eleven miles of walls.

What is harder to estimate is the population of these ancient towns. They were at first limited by the same difficulties in transport as early medieval Western towns, and seem to have had populations of the same order, that is, from about two thousand to twenty thousand people. Probably the normal size of an early city was close to what we would now call a neighborhood unit: five thousand souls or less.

Frankfort, digging in Ur, Eshnunna, and Khafaje, which flourished about 2,000 B.C., found that the houses numbered about twenty to the acre, which gave a density, he calculated, of from 120 to 200 people per acre, a density certainly in excess of what was hygienically desirable, but no worse than that of the more crowded workmen's quarters in Amsterdam in the seventeenth century: in both cases perhaps offset a little by the presence of canals.

Though the size of the typical early city was modest and its scope largely confined to its neighboring region, the scale of the citadel and its chief buildings might verge on the colossal: no sacrifice was too great to enhance its prestige and its power, or to ensure its permanence. Strangely enough, though, some of the earliest cities show physical features in the residential quarters that were lost in the later development of the city, though the rulers might still retain them. The regular street plan, the row houses, the bathrooms and the inside latrines, the pottery pipes, the brick-lined drainage channels in the streets, the culverts to carry off the rainwater—all these the digger finds in the ruins of Mohenjo-Daro and finds again, with minor variations, in spreading Ur or little Lagash.

JOINT EXPEDITION, UNIVERSITY MUSEUM, PHILADELPHIA; ORIENTAL INSTITUTE, CHICAGO

The broad street had come in before the invention of wheeled vehicles, for it was probably first laid out for sacred processions and for marching soldiers. The frequent orientation of the main avenues to the points of the compass perhaps indicates the growing dominance of the sky-gods; this layout sometimes flouted more practical considerations, such as tempering the heat or catching the prevailing winds.

The general appearance of these ancient Mesopotamian cities must have been—as Leonard Woolley pointed out—very much like that of a walled North African city today: the same network of narrow streets or rather, alleys, perhaps no more than eight feet wide, with the same one, two, and three story houses, the same usable roof tops, the same inner courts, and finally, the steep pyramid of the ziggurat dominating it all, as the towers of the mosque now dominate the Moslem city.

THE GREEK POLIS

Greek city development made many promising institutional departures from the original pattern of the city as it had developed both in Mesopotamia and in the Egypt of the Empire. The Greeks, it seemed, had in some degree freed themselves from the outrageous fantasies of unqualified power that Bronze Age religion and Iron Age technology had fostered: their cities were cut closer to the human measure, and were delivered from the paranoid claims of quasi-divine monarchs, with all the attending compulsions and regimentations of militarism and bureaucracy.

As the city developed, the democratic habits of the village would be often carried into its heretofore specialized activities, with a constant rotation of human functions and civic duties, and with a full participation by each citizen in every aspect of the common life. Within a couple of centuries the Greeks discovered more about the nature and potentialities of man than the Egyptians or the Sumerians seem to have discovered in as many millennia. All these achievements were concentrated in the Greek polis, and in particular, in the greatest of these cities, Athens. The core of the city, the center of its most valued activities, the essence of its total existence, was the acropolis. Here are the true sources of the ancient city, from paleolithic spring and cave to neolithic wall and sacred enclosure, from royal palace and fortress to cosmic temple, from protected camp and village to the proud and powerful city.

While these central structures on Athens' Acropolis were still, at the end of the sixth century, extremely simple, often doubtless crude, even when built of stone, one must read an even greater simplicity and roughness into the stalls, booths, and workshops of the agora below, where the sausage seller and the silversmith, the spice merchant and the potter and the money-changer held forth.

If in the fifth-century economy the agora can be properly called a market place, its oldest and most persistent function was that of a communal meeting place. As usual, the market was a by-product of the coming together of consumers who had

MARTIN HURLIMANN—FROM *Eternal Greece*, VIKING PRESS; BELOW: GEORGINA MASSON—FROM *Rome for Ourselves*, MCGRAW-HILL; BOTH, THAMES & HUDSON, LONDON

many other reasons for assembling than merely doing business with one another.

To understand the full achievement of the Hellenic polis, one must take one's eyes off the buildings and look more closely at the citizen. For all the crudeness of the urban setting, as late as the fifth century, the Greek citizen had mastered Emerson's great secret: save on the low levels and spend on the high ones. What we regard too glibly as an unfortunate handicap may in fact be partly responsible for the greatness of Athens.

The Greek citizen was poor in comforts and convenience; but he was rich in a wide variety of experiences, precisely because he had succeeded in by-passing so many of the life-defeating routines and materialistic compulsions of civilization. Partly he had done this by throwing a large share of the physical burden on slaves, but even more by cutting down on his own purely physical demands and expanding the province of the mind. If he did not see the dirt around him, it was because beauty held his eye and charmed his ear. In Athens, at least, the muses had a home.

What distinguished the Greek polis in its developing phase was the fact that no part of its life was out of sight or out of mind. All that men did was open to inspection, alike in the market, the workshop, the law court, the council, the gymnasium; and whatever was natural was acceptable so that the naked body would be proudly shown in athletic contests, and even its most repulsive physiological processes were not excluded from consciousness. In that sense the Greek had a completely open mind. Until Pericles, the intimate human scale was maintained in every quarter, and the whole network of urban activities had visible form and relationship.

For a brief generation in Athens, the ways of the gods, the ways of nature, and the ways of men came close to a common point: it seemed as if the arrests and fixations, the aberrations and perversions embedded almost from the beginning in the very stones of the ancient city might be overcome. In the activities of the polis, if not in all its architectural furniture, human nature suddenly rose to fuller stature.

With its Acropolis dominating the plain below, Athens is the archetypal Greek city. The Acropolis is not only a true citadel, a fortress rock, but also the traditional preserve of the gods, with many ancient shrines as well as the later Parthenon, at right, and the Propylaea, at left. Yet for all its grandeur, Athens was built to human scale, and its chief glory was its free, inquiring citizen. He was applauded by the Romans, who often, as above, showed Greek philosophers on their sarcophagi.

ANDERSON–GIRAUDON; OVERLEAF: ITALY'S NEWS PHOTOS–MUSEO DELLA CIVILTÀ ROMANA

ROME

The Roman Empire, the product of a single expanding urban power center, was itself a vast city-building enterprise: it left the imprint of Rome on every part of Europe, Northern Africa, and Asia Minor, altering the way of life in old cities and establishing its special kind of order, from the ground up, in hundreds of new foundations, "colonial" towns, "free" towns, towns under Roman municipal law, "tributary" towns: each with a different status if not a different form. In a general account of the Roman state just before it fell into ruin, the writer treated it as made up of separate civic bodies, to the number of 5,627. Even after the city of Rome had been sacked in the fifth century A.D., the poet Rutilius Namatianus could say, with undiminished admiration: "A city of the far-flung earth you made."

But Rome never had the imagination to apply the principles of limitation, restraint, orderly arrangement, and balance to its own urban and imperial existence.

Surely it is no accident that the oldest monument of Roman engineering is the Cloaca Maxima, the great sewer, constructed in the sixth century B.C. on a scale so gigantic that either its builders must have clairvoyantly seen, at the earliest moment, that this heap of villages would become a metropolis of a million inhabitants, or else they must have taken for granted that the chief business and ultimate end of life is the physiological process of evacuation. So sound was the stone construction, so ample the dimensions, that this sewer is still in use today. But as frequently happens in the vulgar applications of engineering, the physical benefits were limited by a certain poverty of imagination in carrying them through. The superabundant engineering was inadequate because—as in so much imposing American highway construction today—the human end in view was too dimly perceived or too reluctantly accepted as a final guide. Thus, just as our expressways are not articulated with the local street system, so the great sewers of Rome were not connected with water closets above the first floor. Even worse, they were not connected to the crowded tenements at all. In short, where the need was greatest, the mechanical facilities were least.

As soon as the increase of population created a demand for wheeled traffic in Rome, the congestion became intolerable. One of Julius Caesar's first acts on seizing power was to ban wheeled traffic from the center of Rome during the day. The effect of this, of course, was to create such a noise at night, with wood or iron-shod cart wheels rumbling over the stone paving blocks, that the racket tormented sleep: at a much later date, it drove the poet Juvenal into insomnia.

From the standpoint of both politics and urbanism, Rome remains a significant lesson of what to avoid: its history presents a series of classic danger signals to warn one when life is moving in the wrong direction. Wherever crowds gather in suffocating numbers, wherever rents rise steeply and housing conditions deteriorate, wherever a one-sided exploitation of distant territories removes the pressure to achieve balance and harmony nearer at hand, there the precedents of Roman building almost automatically revive, as they have come back today: the arena, the tall tenement, the mass contests and exhibitions, the football matches, the international beauty contests, the strip tease made ubiquitous by advertisement, the constant titillation of the senses by sex, liquor, and violence—all in true Roman style. So, too, the multiplication of bathrooms and the overexpenditure on broadly paved motor roads, and above all, the massive collective concentration on glib ephemeralities of all kinds, performed with supreme technical audacity. These are symptoms of the end: magnifications of demoralized power, minifications of life. When these signs multiply, Necropolis is near, though not a stone has yet crumbled. For the barbarian has already captured the city from within. Come, hangman! Come, vulture!

EDWIN SMITH

To divert the restless Roman mobs, emperors provided a ceaseless round of public amusements: chariot races, parades, and gladiatorial contests. Even the sanest of emperors, Marcus Aurelius, shown leading a triumph in the relief opposite, felt obliged to attend the bloody orgies of the circus. But Rome's decadence and cruelty sped its fall: at Herculaneum the shape of the future was inscribed (above) by some nameless, secret Christian. When archaeologists unearthed this Roman resort city, they found, in an attic room of a great house, the mark of a cross, once affixed by nails above a rude wooden cupboard which was very likely used as an altar. The triumph of Christianity had begun.

OVERLEAF:
A scale model of Rome in the time of Constantine shows the curve of the Tiber at the far left and the Circus Maximus in the left foreground. Overlooking the Circus is the cluster of palaces on the Palatine hill, from which the emperors could watch the entertainments without ever leaving their terraces. Prominent on the right is the Colosseum, next to it, seen in the foreground, is the temple of Claudius, and behind it are the baths of Titus and Trajan.

MUSEES ROYAUX DES BEAUX-ARTS, BRUSSELS; OVERLEAF: COMPANIE AERIENNE FRANÇAISE

THE MEDIEVAL TOWN

The medieval town was a more thriving biological environment than one might suspect from looking at its decayed remains. There were smoky rooms to endure; but there was also perfume in the garden behind the burghers' houses, for fragrant flowers and herbs were widely cultivated. There was the smell of the barnyard in the street, diminishing in the sixteenth century, except for the growing presence of horses and stables. But there would also be the odor of flowering orchards in the spring, or the scent of the new-mown grain, floating across the fields in early summer.

Cockneys may wrinkle their noses at this combination of rankness and fragrance, but no lover of country ways will be put off by the smell of cow or horse dung. Is the reek of gasoline exhaust, the sour smell of a subway crowd, the pervasive odor of a garbage dump, the sulphurous fumes of a chemical works, the carbolated rankness of a public lavatory, for that matter, the chlorinated exudation from a glass of ordinary drinking water more gratifying? Even in the matter of smells, sweetness is not entirely on the side of the modern town; but since the smells are *our* smells, many of us blandly fail to notice them.

As for the eye and the ear, there is no doubt where the balance of advantage goes. The majority of medieval towns in these respects were immensely superior to those erected during the last two centuries; is it not mainly for their beauty, indeed, that people still make pilgrimages to them? One awoke in a medieval town to the crowing of a cock, the chirping of birds nesting under the eaves, or to the tolling of the hour in the monastery on the outskirts, perhaps to the chime of bells in the new bell tower in the market square, to announce the beginning of the working day, or the opening of the market. Song rose easily on the lips, from the plain chant of the monks to the refrains of the ballad singer in the market place, or that of the apprentice and the housemaid at work. Singing, acting, dancing were still "do-it-yourself" activities.

If the ear was stirred, the eye was even more deeply delighted. Every part of the town, beginning with the walls themselves, was conceived and executed as a work of art; even parts of a sacred structure that might be unseen, were still finished as carefully as if they were fully visible. As Ruskin long ago noted: God at least would bear witness to the craftsman's faith and joy. The buildings, so far from being musty and "quaint," were as bright and clean as a medieval illumination, if only because they were usually whitewashed with lime, so that all the colors of the image makers, in glass or polychromed wood, would dance in reflection on the walls.

Life flourishes in this dilation of the senses. Without it, the beat of the pulse is slower, the tone of the muscles is lower, the posture lacks confidence, the finer discriminations of the eye and the touch are lacking, perhaps the will to live itself is defeated. To starve the eye, the ear, the skin, the nose is just as much to court death as to withhold food from the stomach. Though diet was often meager in the Middle Ages, though many comforts for the body were lacking even for

BRITISH MUSEUM

Processions of Canterbury pilgrims lent color and motion to the medieval landscape of walled cities and cloistered monasteries. Opposite: An imaginary Gothic cathedral, the focus of town life, is portrayed in Jan van Eyck's monochrome painting, Saint Barbara.

those who did not impose penitential abstentions upon themselves, the most destitute or the most ascetic could not wholly close his eyes to beauty. The town itself was an ever-present work of art; and the very clothes of its citizens on festival days were like a flower garden in bloom.

The medieval town was above all things, in its busy turbulent life, a stage for the ceremonies of the church. Therein lay its drama and its ideal consummation. Just as in the late industrial age the imagination showed itself on the highest level in a railroad station or a bridge, in medieval culture practical achievement reached its peak, by an opposite movement, in the service of a great symbol of salvation. Men who had little to eat gave part of that little to say prayers and masses, light candles, and build a mighty fabric, in which legend, allegory, dogma, and knowledge crystallized in nave and altar, in screen and wall painting, in porch and rose window. On isolated occasions of great religious exaltation, such as Henry Adams described in *Mont-Saint-Michel and Chartres,* they might even carry the very stones that were needed to the site, rich and poor alike.

Within the general medieval pattern, deep changes in feeling took place across five centuries. Radically different life-experiences separate the confident sobriety of the great Romanesque building, as solid as a fortress, as solemn as plain chant, from the humanism of the magnificent lady churches, audacious and lightheartedly experimental, where the walled tomb that symbolized acceptance of death turned into a heavenly lantern with its promise of Resurrection.

OVERLEAF: Amid the turmoil of the early Middle Ages, men turned again in self-defense to that current urban safeguard, the wall. Carcassonne in southern France is perhaps the best surviving example of the medieval walled town. Separated from the ville basse *by the river Aude, it was set high on a hill which was originally the site of the Roman fortress of Carcaso. For centuries it was a way station for travelers journeying from the Mediterranean; taken from the Romans by the Visigoths, it was lost to the Arabs, who lost it in turn to Pippin the Short. The ramparts of the old fortress are surmounted by 52 towers, and they can be entered only by two fortified gates to the east and west. Both the cathedral and castle are seen on the right; the houses tightly huddled in the tangle of narrow streets are still inhabited.*

NETHERLANDS INFORMATION SERVICE

THE BAROQUE CITY

The avenue is the most important symbol and the main fact about the baroque city. Not always was it possible to design a whole new city in the baroque mode; but in the layout of half a dozen new avenues, or in a new quarter, its character could be redefined. In the linear evolution of the city plan, the movement of wheeled vehicles played a critical part; and the general geometrizing of space, so characteristic of the period, would have been altogether functionless had it not facilitated the movement of traffic and transport, at the same time that it served as an expression of the dominant sense of life.

Movement in a straight line along an avenue was not merely an economy, but a special pleasure: it brought into the city the stimulus and exhilaration of swift motion, which hitherto only the horseman had known galloping over the fields, or through the hunting forest. It was possible to increase this pleasure aesthetically by the regular setting of buildings, with regular façades and even cornices, whose horizontal lines tended toward the same vanishing point as that toward which the carriage itself was rolling. What would be monotony for a fixed position or even in a procession becomes a necessary counterpoise to the pace of fast-moving horses.

In emphasizing the demands of wheeled traffic, which became urgent in the seventeenth century, I do not wish to neglect a characteristic need that disclosed itself at an even earlier period: the need of avenues for military movement.

The aesthetic effect of the regular ranks and the straight line of soldiers is increased by the regularity of the avenue: the unswerving line of march greatly contributes to the display of power, and a regiment moving thus gives the impression that it would break through a solid wall without losing a beat. That, of course, is exactly the belief that the soldier and the Prince desire to inculcate in the populace: it helps keep them in order without coming to an actual trial of strength, which always carries the bare possibility that the army might be worsted. Moreover, on irregular streets, poorly paved, with plenty of loose cobblestones and places of concealment, the spontaneous formations of untrained people have an advantage over a drilled soldiery: soldiers cannot fire around corners, nor can they protect themselves from bricks heaved from chimney tops immediately overhead: they need space to maneuver in. Were not the ancient medieval streets of Paris one of the last refuges of urban liberties? No wonder that Napoleon III sanctioned the breaking through of narrow streets and cul-de-sacs and the razing of whole quarters to provide wide boulevards: this was the best possible protection against assault from within. To rule merely by coercion, without affectionate consent, one must have the appropriate urban background.

In the medieval town, the upper classes and the lower classes had jostled together on the street, in the market place, as they did in the cathedral. Now, with the development of the wide avenue, the dissociation of the upper and the lower classes achieves form in the city itself. The rich drive; the poor walk.

The daily parade of the powerful becomes one of the principal dramas of the baroque city: a vicarious life of dash and glitter and expense is thus offered to the butcher's boy with a basket on his head, to the retired merchant out for a stroll, to the fashionable housewife shopping for bargains and novelties, to the idle mob of hangers-on in all degrees of shabby gentility and downright misery—corresponding to the clients of imperial Rome.

"Mind the carriages!" cried Mercier in his eighteenth-century *Tableau de Paris*. "Here comes the black-coated physician in his chariot, the dancing master in his *cabriolet*, the fencing master in his *diable*—and the Prince behind six horses at the gallop as if he were in the open country. . . . The threatening wheels of the overbearing rich drive as rapidly as ever over stones stained with the blood of their unhappy victims."

ROBERT DURANDAUD

The little Dutch town of Naarden, opposite top, was captured by the French in 1672 and elaborately fortified according to the baroque "asterisk" plan of Louis XIV's engineer, Vauban; today the outer reaches of the star figure, extending from Naarden's older center, have been converted from fortifications into parks. As used by Mumford, the term "baroque" connotes an urban scheme which usually revolves around a central place or square: the center is dominated by a palace or monument and provides the nucleus for a system of wide avenues, flanked symmetrically by public buildings, extending throughout the city and imposing a rigid geometric design on the whole. In their broad outlines Paris, Washington, Vienna, and Berlin are baroque; their design has been more widely copied than any other in the planning of modern cities. Perhaps the most famous example of the baroque asterisk is the Etoile shown above: with its twelve avenues—one of them the Champs Elysées—radiating from the Arc de Triomphe, it is an ideal theater for marching men and spectators, although it may seem less admirable to motorists or to the pedestrian on his way to the far side. The giddy pace of horses and carriages, provided an ideal setting by the baroque urban scheme, is captured in the engraving at right of London's Hyde Park Corner; in the design of such royal parks the asterisk plan evolved.

RADIO TIMES HULTON PICTURE LIBRARY

CULVER PICTURES, INC.

SQUARE AND CRESCENT

In one place baroque planning rose above its political and military premises. This was in the conception of the residential square. The open square had never disappeared; but by the same token it had never, even in the Middle Ages, been used entirely for residential purposes, if only because the counting-house and the shop were then part of the home. But in the seventeenth century, it reappeared in a new guise, or rather, it now performed a new urban purpose, that of bringing together, in full view of each other, a group of residences occupied by people of the same general calling and position.

In the older type of city, particularly on the Continent, the rich and the poor, the great and the humble had often mingled in the same quarter, and in Paris for instance, they long continued to occupy the same buildings, the wealthier on the ground floor, the poorest in the attic, five or six stories above. But now, beginning, it would seem, with the establishment of Gray's Inn in London in 1600, a new kind of square was formed: an open space surrounded solely by dwelling houses, without shops or public buildings, except perhaps a church.

Architecturally, these squares were at the beginning somewhat bleak; they looked more like a parade ground than the little urban parks many of them became after the eighteenth century, when the romantic taste for landscape came back into the stony wastes of the town. The open spaces of the squares were not conceived, indeed, as places for strolling and relaxing in the open, as they are used now: they were rather, parking lots for vehicles: places, as Evelyn noted in *Londinum Redevivum,* where coaches may stand, and where no doubt the impatient horses on a cold day might be exercised from time to time while the coachman was waiting for his master or mistress. So, ironically, such squares as the Place Vendôme (1677–1701), which now serves as a car-park for automobiles, are in a sense only reverting to their original use: but with this difference—the old coaches were usually limited in number, and many of them would be in motion, whereas the present occupants form a solid, immobile mass.

The example set by London and Paris was imitated in lesser cities. The squares and circles and crescents of Bath, as laid out by the Woods, reached a higher pitch of perfection than elsewhere, perhaps, partly because of a truly magnificent exploitation of the irregular hilly sites in the new parts of the town. Unfortunately, since it is the buildings of the Royal Crescent that are usually photographed, not the view from them, those who have not visited Bath may easily not realize that the wide sweep of the Crescent is not an arbitrary form, but an imaginative response to the wide sweep of landscape that the site commands: a view of the distant hills that must have been even more striking before the intervening trees had grown sufficiently to close it off. Here the baroque prodigality of space was amply justified by the aesthetic result—to say nothing of the salubrity of such open planning.

Two beautiful examples of what Lewis Mumford regards as baroque design are the Place des Vosges in Paris (right) and the Royal Crescent at Bath (below). The Place des Vosges originally had 38 uniform houses and was completely closed to traffic; it now has two entrances for vehicles, but its open square is still intact. The Royal Crescent, situated on a height that commands the whole surrounding valley, is a rare instance of baroque planning in which geometric design was adjusted to geography. A favorite resort of English society, as suggested at left, Bath was "a great mart of folly" to the disdainful Oliver Goldsmith, a mecca for those "people of fashion who had no agreeable summer retreat from the town and . . . wanted some place where they might have each other's company, and win each other's money, as they had done during the winter in town."

ROBERT DURANDAUD

AEROFILMS

VENICE: MODEL FOR ALL CITIES

Venice in its heyday is shown in this engraving of 1500: in its main outlines it is little changed today. A city of some 175 canals, it is dominated by the majestic Grand Canal, which winds slowly through the town in an inverted S. At the waterway's mid-point is the Rialto Bridge; at its lower terminus it gives gracefully onto the heart of Venice: the Doge's Palace and the Piazza San Marco. At right is the enclosed rectangular water basin of the Arsenal, the shipbuilding center for the Venetian fleet; the fleet itself is at anchor in the foreground. The group of five small islands at the top of the map is the glassblowers quarter, Murano, still occupied by these artisans today. To the left foreground is the island of Giudecca, the original Jewish quarter, now the industrial center of Venice.

At the close of the Middle Ages, one city in Europe stood out above every other because of its beauty and its wealth. No other city shows, in more diagrammatic form, the ideal components of the medieval urban structure. In addition, none gave a better indication in its own internal development of a new urban constellation that promised to transcend the walled container, as it had existed from the end of the neolithic phase.

Venice was the creation of a group of refugees from Padua in the fifth century A.D., fleeing across the lagoons from the invader. The shallow waters of the Adriatic took the place of the stone wall for protection, and the swamps and islands, connected only by water, suggested the dredging of canals to fill in the nearby lands and to establish channels of transportation.

At the core of Venice lies the Piazza San Marco: an open space in front of its ancient Byzantine church, originally the orchards of St. Mark's. What the casual tourist often does

not always realize is that the pattern of St. Mark's is repeated on a smaller scale in each of the parishes of Venice. Each has its campo, or square, often of an odd trapezoidal shape, with its fountain, its church, its school, often its own guildhall; for the city was originally divided into six neighborhoods, each harboring one of the six guilds of the city. The canals, now some 177 in all, serve as the boundaries of these neighborhoods, as well as connecting links: they are both waterbelts and arterial highways, functioning like the greenbelts and through motorways of a well-designed modern town.

According to its situation and size, each of Venice's islands found its appropriate function: not least that dedicated to the convent of San Giorgio, close to St. Mark's. The first functional precinct was that of Torcello: a church and a cemetery islet seven miles away, where the dead were buried. The next precinct was an industrial quarter, that of the Arsenal, erected in 1104, enlarged in 1473 and again in the sixteenth century: a shipyard, provisioning center for vessels, and a munitions works, which in the fifteenth century employed 16,000 workmen and harbored 36,000 seamen. Another main industry of Venice, its glass industry, was established by an act of the Grand Council on the islands of Murano by 1255.

Now these were the first large-scale industrial areas to be set apart from the mixed uses of the ordinary medieval city. Had there been eyes to see and intelligence to appraise, Venice might have set the pattern for the development of heavy industries in growing urban centers after the sixteenth century; and as rapid transport facilities increased, the nuclear but open plan of Venice would, if imitated, have overcome the tendency to provide for extension by solid massing and overcrowding and sprawling, in the fashion of other expanding cities.

If people were aware of the uniqueness of Venice's plan, they treated it as a mere accident of nature, not as a series of bold adaptations which, though based on singular natural features, had a universal application. Venice pushed farther, right into our own age, the organization by neighborhoods and precincts whose recovery today, as an essential cellular unit of planning, is one of the fundamental steps toward reestablishing a new urban form.

AMSTERDAM: A FUNCTIONAL PLAN

RIJKSMUSEUM, AMSTERDAM

The graceful, unhurried, uncrowded life of seventeenth-century Amsterdam is shown in the painting above by Gerrit Berckheyde, The Flower Market at Amsterdam. *Such tranquility was no happy accident but the result of foresight and planning. The arrangement of canals, and of buildings along them, was conceived as a unity; by an ordinance of 1565, civic approval was required for each new structure. Thus the burghers of Amsterdam, balancing public and private interests, controlled the city's growth during its centuries of rapid commercial development.*

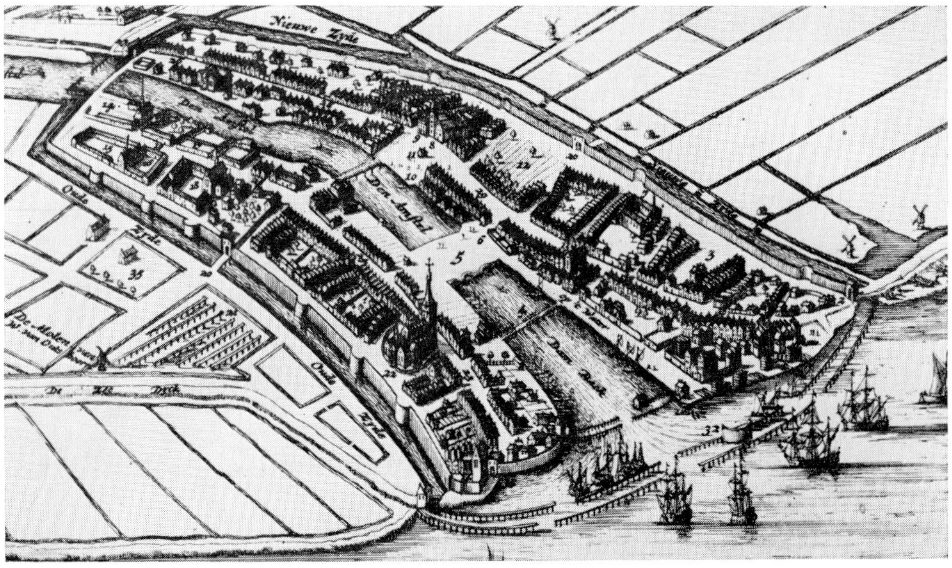

PHOTOGRAPHS COURTESY HARCOURT, BRACE & WORLD, INC.

There is one city that bears witness to the commercial spirit at its best, before it had completely dissociated itself from the customary controls and the collective commitments of its medieval prototype. That city is Amsterdam. The fact that it was not widely imitated shows that it was not capitalism alone, but a complex of institutions, personalities, and opportunities, coming together at a unique moment, that made that city one of the greatest examples of the town planner's art. Even so, it remains capitalism's one outstanding urban achievement, rivaled only by elegant Bath.

Amsterdam began as a community with the diking or damming of the little river, the Amstel. The original urban core was contained within the crescent canal that surrounded the old city, not walled until 1482; but in Dutch cities the dike, in fact, took the place of the wall in promoting cohesion and common effort.

The Plan of the Three Canals is a miracle of spaciousness, compactness, intelligible order. It accepted all that was valid in baroque planning, with just sufficient variation in the individual units, combined with the rich tracery of trees bordering the canals, to take the curse off the military regimentation of baroque classicism. The successive breaks in direction of the spider-web plan keeps the distant vista from being empty and oppressive. The canals themselves were 80 to 88 feet wide: set off by paved, tree-lined walks from the buildings that lined them. These buildings were based on lots that averaged 26 feet in width, thus giving rise to the ample, three-windowed façade, with far more opening than wall, which brought sunlight into the depths of the house. There was a minimum distance of 160 feet between the backs of buildings: and the garden space for each lot was therefore around 26 by 80 feet; a generous space for both lovers of gardens and those who sought outdoor repose. The maximum site coverage was 56 per cent. This plan brought the delights of the suburb, its open space, its gardens, its trees, within the closer compass of the inner city.

Here in the new quarters of Amsterdam was the aesthetic culmination of five centuries of collective effort in commanding water and making land. Order had spread from polders to city. Nothing so thoroughly and uniformly good as Amsterdam had previously made its way into city design, on the same scale, anywhere.

The order created by the Plan of the Three Canals remained in advance of any other urban planning, taken as a whole, for three centuries. It is only now that it is seriously threatened by the religion of the motorcar, which is ready to sacrifice the utilities and delights of city life for the development of space-eating facilities for getting in and out of town—though the very multiplication of such facilities reduces the effective speed of the traffic it seeks to promote. Like the boulevards of Paris, the handsome arbored ways that line the great canals have been reduced to parking lots: a depressing spectacle.

Three stages in the intelligent, ordered development of Amsterdam are seen below. At far left is the original core of the city with the river Amstel entering in the left corner, the old retaining wall on three sides of the city, the main canal down the center, and the sea at the bottom. In the next stage canals have been added on either side of the main canal, windmills built on the wall, and extensive port facilities provided. In the third stage the city has spread farther without losing its logical arrangement of streets and canals.

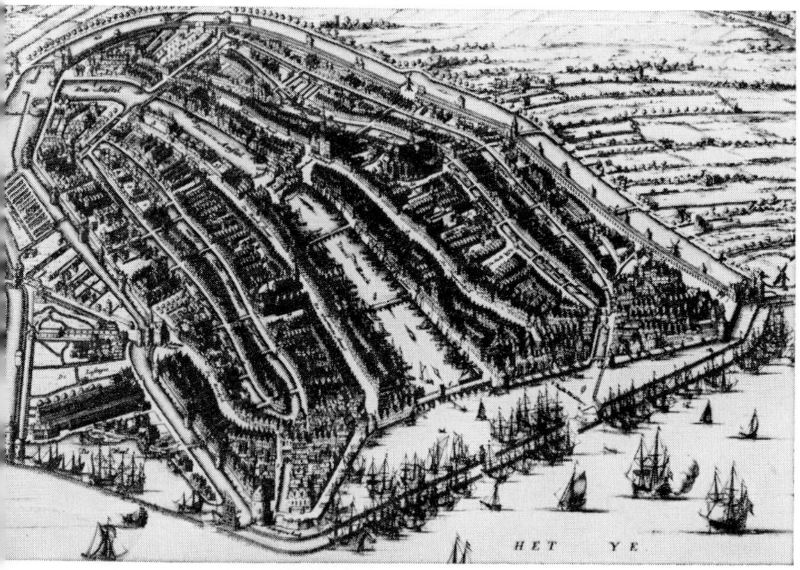

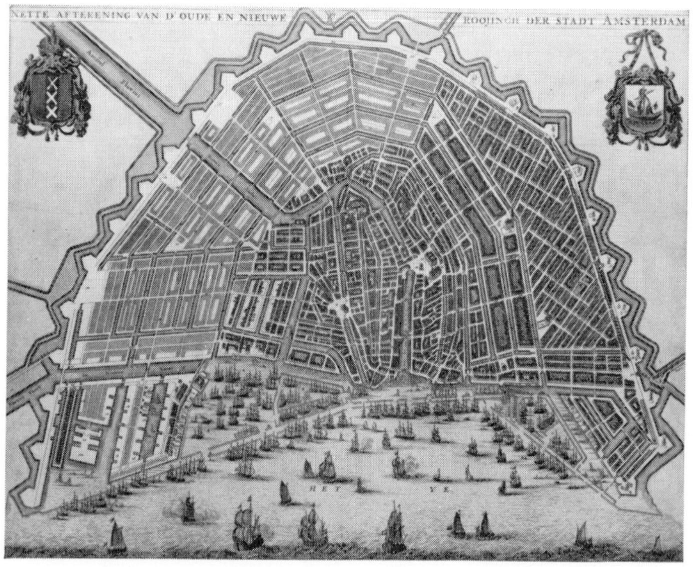

The squalor of life in the sunless industrial slums of London in the 1870's, is portrayed at right in a Gustave Doré engraving. Another example of Coketown at its worst is shown opposite in an air view of Hanley, England, as it appeared before World War II. A jumble of houses and pottery kilns, with polluted waterway and a total lack of greenery, it was, in Lewis Mumford's phrase, "the undertaker's delight." Only because it is Sunday are the kilns not belching black smoke.

N.Y. PUB. LIB. PRINT ROOM

COKETOWN

The change from organized urban handicraft to large-scale factory production transformed the industrial towns into dark hives, busily puffing, clanking, screeching, smoking for twelve and fourteen hours a day, sometimes going around the clock. Between 1820 and 1900 the destruction and disorder within great cities is like that of a battlefield, proportionate to the very extent of their equipment and the strength of the forces employed. In a greater or lesser degree, every city in the Western world was stamped with the archetypal characteristics of Coketown.

The main elements in the new urban complex were the factory, the railroad, and the slum. By themselves they constituted the industrial town: a word that described merely the fact that more than two thousand people were gathered in an area that could be designated with a proper name. Such urban clots could and did expand a hundred times without acquiring more than a shadow of the institutions that characterize a city in the mature sociological sense—that is, a place in which the social heritage is concentrated, and in which the possibilities of continuous social intercourse and interaction raise to a higher potential all the complex activities of men. Except in shrunken, residual forms, even the characteristic organs of the Stone Age city were lacking.

In lieu of any kind of over-all municipal regulation or planning, the railroad itself was called upon to define the character and project the limits of the town. Except in certain parts of Europe where old-fashioned bureaucratic regulations happily kept the railroad stations at the outskirts of the historic city, the railroad was permitted, or rather, was invited, to plunge into the very heart of the town and to create in the most precious central portions of the city a waste of freight yards and marshaling yards, economically justifiable only in the open country. These yards severed the town's natural arteries and created an impassable barrier between large urban segments: sometimes, as in Philadelphia, a veritable Chinese wall.

Night spread over the coal town: its prevailing color was black. Black clouds of smoke rolled out of the factory chimneys, and the railroad yards, which often cut clean into the town, mangling the very organism, spread soot and cinders everywhere. The invention of artificial illuminating gas was an indispensable aid to this spread; for without its aid work would frequently have been stopped by smoke and fog. The manufacture of illuminating gas within the confines of the towns became a characteristic new feature: the huge gas tanks reared their bulk over the urban landscape, great structures, on the scale of a cathedral: their tracery of iron, against an occasional clear lemon-green sky at sunrise, was one of the most pleasant aesthetic elements in the new order.

Such structures were not necessarily evil; indeed, with sufficient care in their segregation they might have been comely. What was atrocious was the fact that, like every other building in the new towns, they were dumped almost at random; the leakage of escaping gas scented the so-called gas-house districts, and not surprisingly these districts frequently became among the most degraded sections of the city. In this new environment black clothes were only a protective coloration, not a form of mourning; the black stovepipe hat was almost a functional design—an assertive symbol of steam power. The black dyes of Leeds, for example, turned its river into a dark poisonous sewer; while the oil smudges of soft coal spat everywhere; even those who washed their hands left a rim of undissolved grease around the side of the washbowl. Add to these constant smudges on flesh and clothing the finely divided particles of iron from the grinding and sharpening operations, the unused chlorine from the soda works, later the clouds of acrid dust from the cement plant, the various by-products of other chemical industries: these things smarted the eyes, rasped the throat and lungs, lowered the general tone, even when they did not produce on contact any definite disease.

Considering this new urban area on its lowest physical terms, without reference to its social facilities or its culture, it is plain that never before in recorded history had such vast masses of people lived in such a savagely deteriorated environment, ugly in form, debased in content.

SUBURBIA: THE END OF A DREAM

Well before the industrial town had taken form the notion of leaving behind the complexities of civilization had become attractive to the European mind once more, just as it had been during the decadence of Rome. For the restless and hardy, there was the conquest and colonization of new lands, mingled with the romantic call of the unspoiled wilderness; for more domestic, reflective souls, there was fishing, rambling, botanizing, going on family picnics, or musing in solitude deep in the woods. Without waiting for Rousseau to prove that most of the ills of life were derived from the arid rituals of an overrefined civilization, many Europeans had begun to act on these premises. Country life seemed best; and the farther one got away from the city the more one gained in health, freedom, independence.

Indeed, the suburb becomes visible almost as early as the city itself, and perhaps explains the ability of the ancient town to survive the insanitary conditions that prevailed within its walls. (Woolley found evidences of suburban developments in "Greater Ur" beyond the built-up area—scattered buildings as far as the temple of al'Ubaid, four miles away.)

By the time maps and air views of late medieval cities were made, we find detailed evidence of little huts, cottages, and villas, with ample gardens, springing up outside the city's walls. By the sixteenth century the land so used served for more than summer residence and recreation. As early as the thirteenth century, indeed, Villani reported that the land for a circle of three miles around Florence was occupied by rich estates with costly mansions; and Venetian families were not behind in their villas on the Brenta. From the beginning, the privileges and delights of suburbanism were reserved largely for the upper class; so that the suburb might almost be described as the collective urban form of the country house—the house in a park—as the suburban way of life is so largely a derivative of the relaxed, playful, goods-consuming aristocratic life that developed out of the rough, bellicose, strenuous existence of the feudal stronghold.

FAIRCHILD AERIAL SURVEYS INC.

To withdraw like a hermit and live like a prince—this was the purpose of the original creators of the suburb. This utopia proved to be, up to a point, a realizable one: so enchanting that those who contrived it failed to see the fatal penalty attached to it—the penalty of popularity, the fatal inundation of a mass movement whose very numbers would wipe out the goods each individual sought for his own domestic circle, and, worse, replace them with a life that was not even a cheap counterfeit, but rather the grim antithesis.

In the mass movement into suburban areas a new kind of community was produced, which caricatured both the historic city and the archetypal suburban refuge: a multitude of uniform, unidentifiable houses, lined up inflexibly, at uniform distances, on uniform roads, in a treeless communal waste, inhabited by people of the same class, the same income, the same age group, witnessing the same television performances, eating the same tasteless prefabricated foods, from the same freezers, conforming in every respect to a common mold, manufactured in the central metropolis. Thus the ultimate effect of the suburban escape in our time is, ironically, a low-grade uniform environment from which escape is impossible.

Only as a nursery for bringing up children did the suburb prove a more adequate environment, particularly in the early days of the railroad suburb, when each settlement was surrounded by a broad greenbelt of woods and fields. Here children could gambol safely, without supervision; and around the suburban schools was play space so ample that it became the ideal requirement for all future schools: space for lawn tennis and croquet, for cricket or baseball, football or bowls. Emerson had noted these advantages clearly in his *Journal*, in 1865: "There is no police so effective as a good hill and wide pasture in the neighborhood of a village, where the boys can run and play and dispose of their superfluous strength and spirits." The suburb established such play space as an essential part of the city: not to be crowded out by high land values. That was a permanent contribution.

But too soon, in breaking away from the city, the part became a substitute for the whole, even as a single phase of life, that of childhood, became the pattern for all the seven ages of man. As leisure generally increased, play became the serious business of life; and the golf course, the country club, the swimming pool, and the cocktail party became the frivolous counterfeits of a more varied and significant life. Thus in reacting against the disadvantages of the crowded city, the suburb itself became an overspecialized community, more and more committed to relaxation and play as ends in themselves. Compulsive play fast became the acceptable alternative to compulsive work: with small gain either in freedom or vital stimulus. Accordingly, the two forms of life blend into each other; for both in suburb and in metropolis, mass production, mass consumption, and mass recreation produce the same kind of encapsulated and denatured environment.

Even children suffered from this transformation of the

A permanent belt of open country is part of the original scheme of Greenbelt, Maryland, a rare example of enlightened planning.

whole community into a mere recreation area. For such a segregated community, composed of segregated economic strata, with little visible daily contact with the realities of the workaday world, placed an undue burden of education on the school and family. The smallest village where people still farm and fish and hunt, the drabbest industrial city whose population still engages in essential productive enterprises, has educational possibilities that the suburb lacks. The operative differences between the contemporary suburb and the big city become increasingly minimal: for in these seemingly different environments reality has been progressively reduced to what filters through the screen of the television set.

The suburb superficially restored the dream of Jeffersonian democracy, almost effaced by the oligarchic proclivities of capitalism, and provided the conditions essential for its success: the small face-to-face community of identifiable people, participating in the common life as equals. Gardening and politics were both "do-it-yourself" activities in the suburb. And just as long as the community retained its natural limitation of area and numbers, it fostered this neighborly life.

The desire for a more genial environment for domestic activities, particularly those of a growing family with the personal responses possible only in a small community, helped to popularize the suburban movement. Unfortunately the suburb itself has lost the conditions that preserved the landscape around it and provided for spontaneous association and common enterprises. What the suburb retains today is largely its original weaknesses: snobbery, segregation, status-seeking, political irresponsibility.

In a recent study in Boston, a survey showed that only one male resident out of three spends any time on community or civic activity in his dormitory suburb. In effect, the suburbanite renounces the obligations of citizenship at both ends; and the farther he goes from the center, the more dissociated he becomes. Neither neighborhood nor city give cohesion to the suburb of the "motor age."

These fast-moving particles are the fallout of the metropolitan explosion. They are no longer held together either by the urban magnet or the urban container: they are rather emblems of the disappearing city. But this movement from the center carries no hope or promise of life at a higher level. Just as our expanding technological universe pushes our daily existence ever farther from its human center, so the expanding urban universe carries its separate fragments ever farther from the city, leaving the individual more dissociated, lonely, and helpless than he probably ever was before. Compulsory mobility provides fewer, not more opportunities for association than compulsory stability provided in the walled town.

What began as a flight from the city by families has become a more general retreat, which has produced not so much individual suburbs as a spreading suburban belt. Under the present suburban regime, every urban function follows the example of the motor road: it devours space and consumes time with increasing friction and frustration, while, under the plausible pretext of increasing the range of speed and communication, it actually obstructs it and denies the possibility of easy meetings and encounters by scattering the fragments of a city at random over a whole region.

The absurd belief that space and rapid locomotion are the chief ingredients of a good life has been fostered by the agents of mass suburbia. The habit of low-density building is the residual bequest of the original romantic movement, and by now it is one of the chief obstacles to reassembling the parts of the city and uniting them in a new pattern that shall offer much richer resources for living than either the congested and disordered central metropolis or the outlying areas reached by its expressways. The *reductio ad absurdum* of this myth is, notoriously, Los Angeles. Here the suburban standard of open space, with free-standing houses, often as few as five houses to the acre, has been maintained: likewise the private motorcar, as the major means of transportation has supplanted what was only a generation or so ago an extremely efficient system of public transportation.

Los Angeles has now become an undifferentiated mass of houses, walled off into sectors by many-laned expressways, with ramps and viaducts that create special bottlenecks of their own. These expressways move but a small fraction of the traffic per hour once carried by public transportation, at a much lower rate of speed, in an environment befouled by smog, itself produced by the lethal exhausts of the technologically backward motorcars. More than a third of the Los Angeles area is consumed by these grotesque transportation facilities: *two-thirds* of central Los Angeles is occupied by streets, freeways, parking facilities, garages. This is space-eating with a vengeance. The last stage of the process already beckons truly progressive minds—to evict the remaining inhabitants and turn the entire area over to automatically propelled vehicles, completely emancipated from any rational human purpose.

THOMAS AIRVIEWS

The ugly monotony of Levittown, a Long Island housing project, is the lot of many of the citizens of the richest country in history.

A Prevalence of

By FRANK GETLEIN

I: Liberals, Let's Face It!

NOTE: The following is a transcript of an address at a private Dutch-treat dinner held after the 1960 election by the Washington branch of Americans for Democratic Activity, a political study and action group. Attendance was limited to the inner echelon of the group. One younger researcher, by the simple expedient of spending three days addressing envelopes, had no difficulty gaining membership in that echelon.

The liberal program in America faces two fundamental, recurring problems: how to get elected and, having got elected, how to carry out the program.

The first part of the problem seems to have been solved, but we would be less than frank if we did not admit, at least to ourselves, that the very solution to the problem of getting elected has added immeasurably to the problem of putting the program into action.

The naïve may ask, "How can this be?" They may wonder what it is, when a political party has received a mandate from the people, that can possibly stand in the way of executing that mandate. The political realist knows all too well.

For the lamentable fact is that there isn't any mandate, there never was, and in all probability there never will be. The only popular mandate really received by a twentieth-century politician was the one given Adolf Hitler. Hitler said well in advance exactly what he was going to do; people voted for him to give him a chance to do it; once elected, he went right ahead and did it.

Things are different over here.

It's a good thing they are different, and I wouldn't have it any other way, but the difference does make it difficult to plan ahead. Take F.D.R. himself. We like to think that he had a mandate; that the people, ground down by the repressive policies of our opposition, rose in rebellion and voted in the NRA, the WPA, the AAA, and most of the rest of the alphabet. It isn't true. All those stirring events of the Hundred Days came up in the Hundred Days and not more than a week or two earlier. I think, myself, people voted for F.D.R. because he had a sculptural head and a voice to go with it.

People voted for Truman because *Life* magazine declared Dewey elected. And Eisenhower! Here the country was swarming with war veterans as never before: you would think the one thing they'd have in common would be a hatred of generals. Yet, in he went, with tremendous majorities, not, I am positive, because people really wanted to rest and relax for eight years—which turned out to be his program—but only because he reminded them of Big Daddy.

Then we come to our recent triumph. Does anyone seriously imagine it was the appeal of the platform that brought the thin margin of victory? I'll tell you what it was: it was the personal misfortune of our opponent that under the hot lights of television he sweat into his make-up.

No, the realistic truth is that the people are too damn dumb to know what's good for them or even what they want. They are not demons, as some have suggested; but they are moved to-and-fro by demons of all descriptions, as the grass in the field is moved by the wind. Our problem is not to build a platform with popular appeal, but to build a platform of our own and attach it to whatever does appeal, pre-eminently a political leader who doesn't sweat.

CONTINUED ON PAGE 68

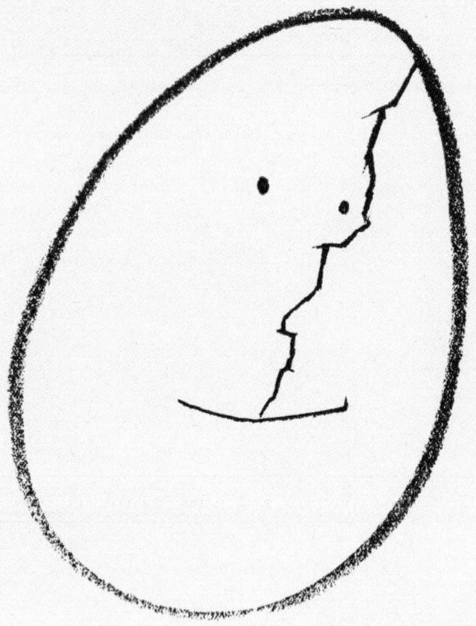

Demons

Modern demons differ from the ghosts and poltergeists of ancestral times, but there are still certain tutelary spirits that hover over the American scene with what seem to be magical powers; often they become the subject of cults. At least this is how Mr. Getlein, a student of our folkways and superstitions, sees it. Here he presents two manifestations: on the left, a message from the all-out liberal side; on the right, a voice from the unreconstructed opposition. Both, along with other researches of the author, a staff writer on the Washington Star *and an art critic as well, will appear this fall in his book* A Modern Demonology.

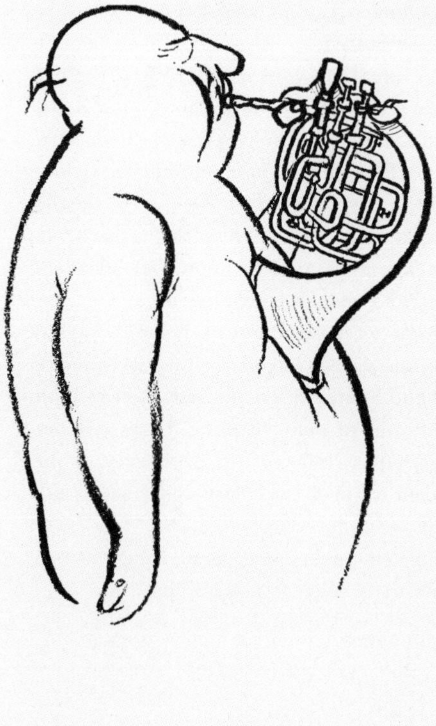

II: Reveille for Reactionaries

NOTE: The following is a transcript of an address at a private $1000-a-plate dinner held after the 1960 election by the Friends of the Republic, a political study and action group. The tape was made by the director himself, the only member of the Demonology Department old enough to seem a likely Friend or a likely diner at such a well-laid table.

I take it we are all in agreement that a sizable majority of the American people are conservative at heart, want a conservative government, and will vote for a conservative President any time they get the chance.

These truths being self-evident, we must face the repugnant fact that in 1960 the American people elected a liberal candidate and turned down our own offering. Furthermore, projections of present political alignments in the states make it all too clear that that performance will be repeated again and again except when we can get a nonpolitical—and therefore nonconservative in any real sense—figure to head up the party's ticket.

How can these two opposing sets of apparent truths be reconciled? Or, to come down off the high plane of philosophy and into the realm of the practical, how can we manage to get elected again? To this question I shall address myself tonight.

In the first place, I think we must face squarely the fact that we are ourselves largely responsible for the liberal victory of 1960 and for the resulting distress we now find ourselves in nationally. Our responsibility goes back to the heady year of 1947, when we found ourselves, for the first time since Hoover, in control of Congress. I shall not rehearse the genuine accomplishments of that Congress: they are too well known, sometimes I think much too well known, to need repetition. But gentlemen, we stooped to folly in backing the Twenty-second Amendment to the Constitution, which forbids a President to succeed himself more than once.

As usual, we were acting from the highest of motives. We wished not to take our long overdue revenge on Franklin Roosevelt, but rather to record for history the country's *real* reaction—hidden by the one-sided majorities he received in elections—to Roosevelt's career. What we all forgot was that Roosevelt was already dead and beyond the reach of our punitive action, except for posthumous impeachment, which, you remember, failed to get a majority in the party caucus.

Well, here we are: we've saved the country from Roosevelt but we've also saved it from ourselves. Without the Twenty-second Amendment and with the astonishing geriatric advances being made by modern medicine—by free-enterprise, conservative medicine—we might have successfully run Eisenhower for another twenty-five years. And in that time surely *someone* else would have turned up.

As I've traveled about the country since the recent disaster, party workers everywhere have asked me if I think Mr. Eisenhower's golf had any effect on the election. I am afraid it did. No one can ever tell me the American people will resent one of their leaders who shares their own wholesome interest in sports, but golf may have been a mistake. We undoubtedly carried the country-club vote, but there is sound reason to think we could have carried that vote with mahjong—a game which, incidentally, might just have brought out the

CONTINUED ON PAGE 69

DRAWINGS BY ROBERT OSBORN

Liberals, Let's Face It! CONTINUED FROM PAGE 66

When we move from the people, victims of the demons, to the demons themselves, still inhabiting our society, we don't have very far to look. We don't even have to go outside our own party. Foremost among the demons are the Southerners—by which, naturally, I mean the white Southerners.

It is at once the disaster and the salvation of liberalism in America that white people in the South still identify our opponents with Abraham Lincoln, despite the fact that Lincoln was a liberal if there ever was one. Consequently, when they go to the polls, they vote, with basic unanimity, against Lincoln and for us. In Presidential elections this automatically gives us a comfortable bloc of electoral votes. In the Senate and the House of Representatives the anti-Lincoln vote normally gives us party control of both houses. This is all to the good and ought to insure the regular passage of liberal legislation in all fields.

Nothing of the sort happens. In session after session liberalism proposes and the South disposes. When the chips are down, the only thing we can really count on from the South is the quadrennial anti-Lincoln vote. The rest of the time they're all Republicans, though they can't admit it. Actually, if the G.O.P. changed its name—to Whigs, perhaps, or Anti-Federalists—and gave us Lincoln, Jacob Javits, and perhaps Nelson Rockefeller, they could carry the South tomorrow.

Happily, this is unlikely.

Difficult as are the demons of the South, there's one thing to be said for them: they're down there, and we're up here. This redeeming grace does not apply to the other great crew of demons within the party, the big-city bosses of the North.

It's all very well to be sentimental and pretend that modern liberalism grew out of the old-time boss and his jobs for people's down-and-out relatives, his grocery baskets at Christmas time, and the annual organization picnic up the river. This happens not to be true. The only thing that grew out of the old-time boss is the new-time boss, and he's no improvement. He doesn't give a damn for liberalism or anything else. All he wants is to get his followers into jobs, both elective and appointive, and to run the city to suit himself. From time to time he uses the city to run the state, and every so often he tries to use the state to run the country. The whole program of liberalism, to him, is a cheap and modern substitute for the old-time grocery baskets.

By all the laws of history the city boss should have been dead and gone when such liberal programs as Social Security, unemployment insurance, and old-age assistance became a matter of law rather than patronage. Instead, he's stronger than ever. Not needing graft the way he used to, he's not even liable to investigation any more. He just goes around shaking hands with people who shake hands with other people, and they all vote as they're told. There's no discussion, there's no dialogue, there's no fruitful exchange of views.

How can you educate people for democracy that way?

When all the sins and shortcomings of the party are acknowledged, however, we are faced with the fact that the real demons are still those on the outside, members of the opposition or the financial and industrial power behind the opposition—the mill owners and monopolists of America. They're a slick bunch, and you have to watch them every minute.

This shows clearly even in recent developments of what may be called the corporate silhouette. In days gone-by the American industrialist was easy to recognize and natural to hate. He wore a high silk hat, smoked a big cigar, and had a great fat belly covered by a vest embroidered with dollar signs. This has all changed. Today's exploiter of the masses keeps himself in good physical shape, wears expensive but tasteful clothes, and is not immediately distinguishable from his better-paid employees. Worse still, he's had a decent education, reads books, goes to the theater, buys paintings, and attends the opera to hear the music. This is protective coloration of the most deliberate sort, and, I am sorry to say, it works.

Personal camouflage of this kind is only the surface manifestation of the same thing going on deep within the corporate labyrinths. One of the great burdens borne by liberals in America is that when we win, we lose. Thus when we got minimum-wage laws passed and people were able to earn enough to live decently, their first reaction was to vote Republican to show that they were respectable now. With industry and finance we've had the same bitter fruits of victory. Years ago, after frightful battles, we legislated a certain minimum of honesty into banks and factories. Do we get credit for this? No, today's money man, operating within the strict supervision we placed upon him, proudly proclaims his honesty.

"I'm no scoundrel," he says, and people believe him because he's right. The point, however, is that his grandfather *was* a scoundrel, and he ought to be hounded for it until the means of production are in the hands of the people, that is, of ourselves.

It's quite true that during the lean years when Eisenhower reigned most of us moved out of the White House into the great foundations. The result is that the foundations themselves have taken on a strongly liberal cast, but the result of *that* is that people give credit not to the tax laws that made foundations inevitable, but to the tycoons and operators who made all the money in the first place and who left their names inseparably linked with the loot for public purposes.

There is no doubt that the people really want liberalism in the years before us. Our task is to make them understand that they want it. As to the nationalizing of industry, we are already well along that path. Increasingly, industrial income is going into the foundations, and increasingly the foundations are becoming a branch of the government—limited, so far, to information and analysis. The breakdown in Soviet-American friendship was a traumatic shock to many of us, but it may yet prove the vital occasion for the absorption of the few remaining areas of industry not already foundationized.

We are thus confronted with the great obstacles to the liberal program: the party in the South and the party in the Northern cities. The only major sector of the party we're really sure of is the party on the campus, and the trouble with the party on the campus is that most of the members aren't old enough to vote.

What we need above all is some way to keep the voting support of the city's bosses and the Southern mosses, but to keep both firmly out of policy making. Unless we are prepared to settle for the presidency of the student council, we must continue to use both, as in the past.

The emerging question of Liberalism in America is, Who is using whom?

Reveille for Reactionaries

CONTINUED FROM PAGE 67

silent conservative majority. The total golf vote is more complex and may well have gone for the liberal candidate, especially in view of the universal experience of American youth with touch football.

My own feeling is that what we really need the next time out is a damn good bowler.

The foregoing observations have been necessary and, I trust, salutary reminders that to err is human and that we ourselves—whatever the opposition may say—are human. We have made errors, and they must be rectified. But actually, there seems little doubt that our consistent record of defeat at the hands of the liberals can only be due to the operation of demons in the Republic. Demons are at large among our opposition, among their labor support, and even among the electorate.

It has been suggested by some that there are demons loose in the American press. I agree. There seems to be no reason for doubting that most American newspapermen are liberal themselves and unquestionably lend a liberal coloring to their reports. But after all, we do have this end of things covered. If reporters are liberal, their employers are, almost to a man, conservatives. The newspaper publishers of America are among our most loyal supporters. It would be base ingratitude to hit them where it hurts. Yet the only way to change the liberal thinking of most reporters would be to raise their pay—a dangerous innovation that might or might not help the party but that would certainly injure the party's publishers.

Nor can I seriously entertain the notion that demonic reporters can be effectively disciplined by the loss of their employment. In the unlikely event that they really did leave the profession, they would all join the faculties of journalism schools, where their ultimate influence would be multiplied many times.

Closer examination reveals the demons of the press to be massed and most effective at the other end of the business—the consumers. Analysis of the returns shows city after city in which the voters, from sheer perversity, cast their ballots directly opposite to the way they were instructed by the press. This tendency was especially strong in those cities where both papers are published by the same member of our party's National Committee.

Difficult as it will be for all, there is only one solution. We must persuade a sizable proportion of our publishers to adopt the liberal line, and thus get newspaper readers as antagonistic to liberalism as they are now to conservatism.

In the excitement of watching the closeness of the popular vote in the 1960 election, some members of the party have come out for reform of the Electoral College. Some have even come out for the abolition of the College, backing the harebrained scheme of having the President elected by the majority of the voters.

I cannot warn you strongly enough against this madness. If we start going in for direct, popular election, the party is finished, at least until we can solve the master political riddle of our century—how to get the conservative majority to vote. You are all aware that we are more or less a permanent minority in both houses of Congress. We would be a much smaller minority if seats in that body all represented the same number of voters. On the other hand, we manage to maintain at least a veto power in most of the state legislatures: that, too, rests firmly on the lucky fact that the votes of country conservatives are worth from twice to four or five times the votes of liberals in the cities. Regardless of an occasional Presidential fluke, the last thing in the world we can afford is electoral reform. Cling to the College; if possible, make it even less representative of the people's voice than it is.

At last we must come to the real demons who defeated us in the late unpleasantness. These are, of course, the labor bosses and their organized minions scattered through the big cities and the heavily industrialized areas. The bosses have been after us for years. It is now apparent that in the last half-dozen elections their techniques have become more effective. The crux of the whole union strategy has been to get people to register and then to get them to vote. For some reason, the unions take it for granted that most people, if they vote at all, will vote liberal. They are right, of course, because the great conservative majority has simply been staying home on election day, in impressive but, alas, ineffective protest against the graduated income tax.

Against this vicious campaign of the unions to get people registered and voting, there is little we can do openly, since we are committed, through the advertising association, to the idea that voting is a patriotic duty.

What can be done otherwise, is another matter. If, instead of aiming another blow at ourselves through Electoral Reform, we pushed elector*ate* reform, we might be able to unfasten the grip the demons of the unions seem to have upon the voters. It has been mentioned by some party theorists that old Federalist thought included a property qualification for voters. Since some of our strongest supporters are not property owners in the strict, realty, Federalist sense, it has been proposed to restrict suffrage to those of a proper income. A dangerous proposal. I ask you only to compare the income of the average steelworker with that of the average bank clerk and ask yourselves who would suffer. The fact is that union labor could meet almost any financial test we could reasonably propose.

What is really wanted is some way to forbid the vote to members of unions. In many a state legislature we have the votes to put such laws through, and our lawyers are already studying the defense against the Supreme Court.

You understand, of course, that all these discussions of strategy are interim proposals. All become academic on the day we finally attract the conservative majority out of their political apathy and into the polls. On that day of wrath, even liberal dogcatchers—with their everlasting cant about finding the hound a home—will be swept out of office.

That day, as we have learned so often, is not yet. We cannot lose faith that it will come. I know that recent statistics of voting have been used to "prove" that the silent conservative majority does not exist. I say those statistics only prove the conservatives are even more silent than we thought. When figures seem to show that almost all the voters have voted and most of them voted for our opponents, those figures really mean that the conservatives have so lost heart that not only do they not vote, not only do they not register to vote, they do not even record the fact of their birth.

And who can blame them?

BLUME'S OAK

The dead skeleton of an ancient Roman tree inspires an American painter to

In an age when most painters spend no more than a few weeks or days on a picture—if that—and number their output in the hundreds, Peter Blume has been known to devote several years to a single work: as he admits, "My large paintings can practically be counted on the fingers of your hand." Since 1929, he has completed only six canvases that he considers "major" both in size and thematic content; his entire output during that period probably numbers no more than several dozen paintings of any kind.

He is famous for his vast, meticulously detailed and often fantastic allegories, which display all the technical craftsmanship of an old master. Three years in gestation, his newest work, *Tasso's Oak* (see following pages), is typical of his special blend of symbolic form and realism that almost recalls the religious painters of the Renaissance.

Tasso's oak is an actual monument in Rome. Now dead and held up by iron girders and masonry (see photograph, page 75), it was once a great spreading tree on the Janiculum, not far from the Vatican. Here the famous Italian poet of the sixteenth century, the half-mad wanderer Torquato Tasso, was supposed to have sat and meditated during the last year of his life, as he waited for Pope Clement VIII to crown him with the laurels that were to be the reward for his greatest work, the heroic epic poem *Jerusalem Delivered*.

The remnants of Tasso's oak—or rather, a generalized representation of them, for Blume has never felt constrained by the limits of strict naturalism—occupy the center of the huge, seven-by-eight-foot canvas. In the shattered and decaying arms of the tree, supported by halo-shaped pieces of girderwork, there is a suggestion of the Crucifixion, a visual metaphor that is not altogether unintentional. From the base of the monument, a single living branch reaches out like a snake emerging from under the brick foundation: as in all Blume's paintings, there is a constant interplay between the old and the new, the dead past and the living present.

Seated around the tree are three women, knitting. "As far as they are concerned," Blume says, "I wasn't thinking of the three Fates—contrary to the supposition of some of my critics. The women are perfectly naturalistic figures. When I was in Italy last, I did a great many drawings of women sitting in the winter sun: during the warm afternoon gossip time, they all gather around public places like this. There is a reason, too, for the headdresses. You see, the women seem to think the sun is very unhealthy, so they pile and wind things around their heads to protect them. . . . Also, in the general scheme of the painting, there is something important

create a fantastic allegory of life

By ROBERT COWLEY

in the fact of knitting—as if the articulation of one stitch with another was a continuation of the creative process itself."

This theme of regeneration is echoed over and over again in *Tasso's Oak*—in the single living branch, in the knitting women, in the little boy chalking a figure of the sun on the pavement, in the lovers ascending the steps of the Janiculum. It is the thread that runs through all Blume's work of the last decade or more. In another major painting, *The Rock,* completed after the end of World War II, a blasted, blood-red boulder is surrounded by symbols of destruction: gutted buildings, skeletons, and burning debris. But even from decay life emerges: from a dead and rotten stump, a beautiful scarlet fungus grows. And everywhere among the ruins, people are at work, rebuilding. "Ever since *The Rock,*" Blume explains, "I've been painting the phoenix, the Resurrection theme, in various forms. And in that sense, I suppose, one is always painting the same picture."

For Peter Blume, many influences worked around *Tasso's Oak*. During 1958, while living at the American Academy in Rome, he constantly wandered about the city, using his car as a studio. "Sometimes a precise sketch or a fragment inspires you to think of other connections," he explains. "Sometimes a unifying idea comes to you in the middle of the night—there is always a moment when everything falls together in a kind of pattern, when you 'see' the entire conception of a picture." The sight of the battered monument on the Janiculum was, perhaps, such a catalyst. Perhaps, too, there was something in the words of the plaque under the skeleton of the tree that assumed special meaning for him. With the florid sentiment that comes so naturally to Italians, it read: ". . . close to his yearned-for laurels and his death Torquato Tasso thought silently again of all his miseries . . . and among the joyful cries made himself knowingly a child among the children."

In the three years that followed, the painting gradually evolved through a unique creative process. Once the idea for it was fixed in his mind, Blume made some three or four hundred rough sketches of the picture. Sometimes only one small detail would be altered; or perhaps some new juxtaposition of line would give him a fresh approach. Then came innumerable drawings of individual details, leading up to a large charcoal-sketched cartoon, almost the size of the completed canvas. Only after a year of this preliminary work did Blume actually begin painting.

At this stage, the problems that remained were mostly

TEXT CONTINUED ON PAGE 74

In its finished state, Peter Blume's canvas Tasso's Oak *owes more to the painter's imagination than to the battered, iron-braced relic that inspired it (see photograph on page 75). The tourist who seeks out the historic tree on the Janiculum will find that it has actually been shored up in rather haphazard fashion, that it does not stand in a spacious terrace as depicted here, and that the splendid Roman panorama behind the parapet is a composite invented by the artist. But Blume used the oak and its environs only as a starting point, a suggestion around which to develop an allegory of decay and regeneration. In the process of working it out he made hundreds of preliminary sketches and drawings, of which only a few details—such as the woman's head and the two nuns on the preceding pages—found their way into the final version of the painting.*

TEXT CONTINUED FROM PAGE 71

those of color and light and texture: "From the beginning, there were several elements that I was trying to relate—behind the hard steel girders holding up the decaying tree, for instance, I wanted a loose, luminous, flowing sky." Another problem was the relationship of the hard green of the braces and the soft green of the new shoots of the living branch: here, an element in the sky was needed to combine them. Again, against such essentially static features as the triangle of masonry and the staircase, Blume introduced another pattern—the design that runs from the children to the lovers and the nuns, and from the nuns to the sky. In this latter motif, a completely new movement was brought into the picture, but one that had to be accomplished with light as much as with pure form. Thus, as the painting developed, it was the sky that held it together.

ROBERT COWLEY

Peter Blume works at so deliberate a pace that his major paintings are separated from each other by several years. The last before Tasso's Oak *was* Passage to Etna, *dated 1957.*

In an age when abstraction is everywhere in vogue, Blume has never once altered his style to suit the mood of the time. This strong sense of independence, of individualistic effort apart from any movement, has always been a distinct pattern in his life. "I have a sense of working alone," he has written, "but I am not unmindful of a common goal. . . . When I started painting in the twenties, I felt that the revolution of modern art emanating from cubism was a crusade to rebuild the fundamental structure of art—its form and color which had been dissipated by naturalism. . . . Later on, by way of dada-surrealism, I saw in the non-naturalistic juxtaposition of pictorial images a correlative with cubism." Blume still considers these two movements the most significant in the art of this century; certainly their influence has long been felt in his work.

Blume was born in Russia in 1906; he came to America at the age of five. His father had taken part in the anti-Czarist revolution of 1905–07 and fled Russia a hunted man. Eventually, Blume's family settled in a poor and predominantly immigrant neighborhood in Brooklyn. After graduating from grade school, he took his first job, working in a lithographic engraving house. Already art was an interest that amounted to an obsession. "I didn't want to go to high school," he relates. "I felt I didn't have any time to lose. Then the truant officers came after me."

As soon as he turned fourteen, however, Blume took out his working papers. During the following years he held a great variety of jobs while he studied painting. He worked briefly as an errand boy in a jewelry factory, ran a subway newsstand, waited on table in Borsch Belt summer hotels, or posed as an artist's model.

It was in the early thirties that Peter Blume first achieved widespread recognition—and at the same time established himself as a rebel among artists. His paintings of this period, a kind of social surrealism highly critical of the mechanized society of the modern world, outraged art critics and public alike—but also earned him in 1932 the Guggenheim fellowship which took him to Italy for the first time. To that country he has returned again and again ("Italy is very stimulating, very beautiful, very dramatic—a fertile, exciting place. I love the light and landscape of Italy"), and it has provided him with the subject matter for many of his major works. The most important result of his first sojourn there was the painting *Eternal City,* which in 1937 was banned by the Corcoran Gallery of Art in Washington for its vicious caricature of Mussolini as a garish green jack-in-the-box springing from the ruins of the Roman Forum.

The early thirties was also the time when Blume settled permanently in western Connecticut, an area that has always attracted people in the arts (see "The Housatonic" in HORIZON for May, 1960). He first lived in a rambling old house on a backwoods road in the small and then remote town of Sherman. In the same building, the poet Hart Crane rented an apartment; Allen Tate and his wife, the writer Caroline Gordon, stayed there from time to time; and Malcolm Cowley lived just down the road. Later, Blume bought a house of his own in Sherman, a high, square, remodeled barn situated in the middle of two beautifully manicured acres. There is a great deal of Blume's character in his property, with its terraces, home-grown *bon-sai* trees, a zucchini-shaped pond, and a profusion of shade elms and rock gardens and bird feeding stations.

After thirty years, Peter Blume remains a controversial figure in American art. And yet, no matter how much paintings like *Tasso's Oak* stand apart from the mainstream of American art today, Blume is not totally out of sympathy with the current abstract movement. "I like the pictures of the so-called 'abstract expressionists' very much," he comments. "I don't feel I'm in competition with them at all. But my concept of a picture is entirely different from theirs. I realize that there *is* an advantage in doing a picture without premeditation—but it's not my style of work. . . . I believe in incorporating in a painting all that you can get into it. Most paintings today have too many elements filtered out of them. I've used ideas in the same way that today many painters use hard and soft colors. Some people think paintings shouldn't have ideas at all."

But Blume finds that for all the new vistas that have been opened in recent years, the whole tendency of modern art is both a limited and limiting form of visual experience, "lacking the pictorial elements and illusions that, until now, good painting has always had."

"A blot is not stimulating to me," Blume remarks. "I wouldn't want to capitalize on it—though sometimes the juxtaposition of a blot or a smudge with another color can be very beautiful, and I fully realize that. In my painting, however, I try to arrive at a total experience that brings together as much as I can encompass in the framework of a single picture. That's why I can't attempt the other thing seriously—and that's why I paint the way I do."

As a neighbor of Peter Blume, Robert Cowley watched the oak grow. He is an assistant editor of AMERICAN HERITAGE.

ALINARI

This is Tasso's oak as it really looks—considerably less dramatic than in Blume's painting, but with the same strange serpentine branch thrusting out from beneath the brickwork.

THE MADNESS AT MONK'S PLACE

The miniature late-evening satirical revue—an art form long favored on the European continent but rarely heretofore popular in America—seems now to be establishing itself here, chiefly through the ministrations of the entrepreneur Julius Monk. Monk (seen at far left, opposite) is a kind of vest-pocket Ziegfeld whose nightly cabaret at what he calls the "Upstairs at the Downstairs," in a converted mansion on New York's West Fifty-sixth Street, presents young talents on a spree of irreverent lampooning of a foolish world in sketch and song.

Monk's current attraction (set in the narrow theater-room over the downstairs bar) is called "Dressed to the Nines," and in the photograph opposite its six performers are grouped on the staircase in key situations from their acts. In ascending order they are Ceil Cabot, singer of splendidly goofy songs; Gordon Connell, here, as gamekeeper, offering a bunny to a supine Lady Chatterley (Lovelady Powell); Mary Louise Wilson, being subjected to a TV quiz on radioactive laundry by Gerry Matthews; at top, Bill Hinnant, brandishing a fan and a toothpick-bat in a wondrously deranged Kabuki burlesque of *Casey at the Bat*. The sketch that includes the Wilson-Matthews duo is the highpoint of the show; in it, writer Ernest Chambers, assisted by all six artists opposite, imagines what it might be like if the government, trying to get its message across to the people, adopted the style of current TV commercials. Below, the script of this sardonic act:

"A WORD FROM OUR SPONSORS"

CHORUS: (*to the tune of the Pepsi-Cola jingle*)
Social security hits the spot,
Forty-five a week, that's a lot,
Extra cash for the kiddies, too—
The Welfare State is the state for you.
Nickel, nickel, nickel, nickel, trickle, trickle, trickle . . .

ANNOUNCER: It's been said that the United States could have the greatest propaganda machine in the world, if we would only make use of the great brains of our advertising industry. Well, this year our government is giving it a try. Here, now, are the first commercials turned out by Madison Avenue to get the television audience behind the policies of the United States government at home and abroad.

ANNOUNCER: Now, from romantic Geneva, comes an exciting new idea in . . . disarmament . . . fashioned with *you* in mind, by four, think of it, *four* of the biggest names on the international scene: jolly, quick-witted Khrush Khrushchev (you saw him on television and you loved him); suave, aristocratic Charles de Gaulle, a *true* Frenchman; Harold MacMillan, NATO's beloved Limey-Primey; and Mr. Ike Eisenhower—*he* was the President of the United States.

This is disarmament with a capital D, the kind you yourself would have designed . . . smart, convenient, *and* easy on the pocketbook. You'll go for disarmament . . . direct to you, and *only* you, from Geneva. It's . . . *disarming*!

CHORUS: Countdown—four, three—countdown—two, one: (*to the tune of the Winston cigarette jingle*)
Tiros works good like a satellite should,
Tiros works good like a (*bleep-bleep*) satellite should.

ANNOUNCER: What do the Turks do when stricken with the everyday agonies of graft, injustice, and corruption in high places? Watch this demonstration. When graft, injustice, and corruption strike, they leave you worn out, depressed, nerves on edge. Ordinary political systems work *one* way, bring just one-way relief. But Democracy acts *three* ways, to 1) stop tiresome graft, 2) quiet depressing injustice, 3) put an end to nerve-jangling corruption. Remember, there is only one genuine Democracy. Don't be fooled by imitations. The next time you get that tired, overrun feeling, do as the Turks do—THROW UP YOUR GOVERNMENT. Take Democracy . . .

CHORUS: Uhm, hmm. What a political system! (*to the tune of the Chevrolet jingle*)
See the Russian view
In a new U-2,
The CIA is calling you today—
SMACK! (*throwing kiss*)

ANNOUNCER: Now, Mrs. Jones, what seems to be the problem?
HOUSEWIFE: It's my husband, Mister, he just lost his job because of his race, creed, and/or national origin.
ANNOUNCER: (*to audience*) A common problem among minority sufferers. But now you can lick this problem and be your old self again with (*holding up "product"*) Bill of Rights, and its amazing new miracle ingredient, P.L. 49—P.L. 49, the new, improved civil-rights measure just passed in Washington. Bill of Rights with P.L. 49 acts instantly to relieve upset. P.L. 49 works like an invisible shield. Watch. (*Holds up atomizer can; sprays between himself and glowering "mob."*) When bigoted hatemongering meanies attack you, P.L. 49 goes to work like this (*raps invisible shield*) invisible shield to give you round-the-clock protection. As you can see, sticks and stones may break your bones, but names will never hurt you . . . not with Bill of Rights! Makes *you* . . . one of the bunch!
VOICE: One of the bunch!
CHORUS: *One of the bunch!*

ANNOUNCER: Hi there, I'm Bob Price down here at the Los Alamos atomic proving ground. Would you mind telling us your name, please, ma'am?
HOUSEWIFE: I'm Mrs. Harvey Jowett of Roanoke, Virginia.
ANNOUNCER: Would you stand over here, Mrs. Jowett, and tell us, have you ever seen either of these two sets of towels before?
HOUSEWIFE: No, I haven't . . . Bob.
ANNOUNCER: (*to audience*) Well, we're going to try a little experiment here. One of these towels comes from a test area where the Soviet government recently exploded a nuclear bomb. The other comes from a test area where *our* government recently set off a bomb. Now, I'm going to ask Mrs. Jowett to look them over carefully and tell us which set of towels is *less radioactive*.
HOUSEWIFE: (*Takes a Geiger counter; it clicks wildly over one pile.*) These . . . this pile.
ANNOUNCER: Let's see which you picked . . . the U.S. or the U.S.S.R. (*flipping over laundry to look at cards beneath the piles*). The U.S.! Less radioactive! *Proof* that U.S. bombs are cleaner by far—even *cleaner* than clean!
HOUSEWIFE: That's certainly the way I'd like *my* towels to look after a nuclear explosion. . . .

Photograph by PHILIPPE HALSMAN

Painted for the King, this finest of Van Dyck's portraits of Charles I now hangs in the Louvre. How it got to France after the King was beheaded is not clear, but the Louvre acquired it when its last royal owner, Louis XVI, suffered a similar fate.

THE PRINCE OF PATRONS

Few men have ever amassed such a treasure in art as the ill-fated Charles I of England, whose dazzling collection became dispersed all over Europe after his doom—to bear witness down to our own day to his superlative taste

By C. V. WEDGWOOD

Everyone knows that King Charles I of England had his head cut off. The unenviable distinction of being the first monarch to be condemned to death by a court consisting of his own subjects has assured him of a lasting but dismal fame. When they assess his character, historians usually admit that whatever his political failings, he had respectable domestic virtues and serious intellectual tastes. Sometimes they add that he was a patron of the arts and a collector of pictures. But his outstanding merits in the one sphere where he was preeminently gifted are, in general, appreciated only by specialists in the art history of England. His achievement, ephemeral though it was, deserves to be better known, not only in justice to him but because the story of the rise and fall of one of the greatest picture collections of the world is full of interest in itself.

In the time of King Charles many European rulers and nobles patronized the arts. But Peter Paul Rubens, who knew and worked for most of them, described King Charles as the greatest connoisseur of them all. The size and quality of the collection he made during his prosperous years, from about 1625 to 1638, entitle him to rank not merely among the great collectors of his age but among the greatest in the world. For a few brief years he assembled on the walls of his palaces in and near London scores of paintings which are today among the most famous treasures of the great European galleries. At Vienna, in the Louvre, and in the Prado the visitor may see today the works of Raphael and Leonardo da Vinci, of Titian, Giorgione, and Tintoretto, of Veronese and Caravaggio, of Holbein, Rubens, and Van Dyck, which once belonged to King Charles and which were sold after his death by the Puritan leaders who had brought him to the block.

To bring such a collection to England, a country in which patronage and collecting were then in their infancy, was an amazing achievement. Yet King Charles, as a collector and patron of the arts, can hardly be said to have had a propitious start. He was born in 1600 in Scotland, a country remote from the warm stream of Mediterranean culture. Three years later, on the death of Queen Elizabeth I, his father ascended the throne of England, and the royal family moved southward to the richer and more populous country. But England at this time had no more tradition than Scotland in the art of painting. Poetry, drama, and music flourished, but in the visual arts the English lagged behind their neighbors in France and Flanders and their rivals, the Spaniards. Italy's generous creative influence in the arts had hardly yet reached their shores, and since the death of Holbein sixty years before, no major European artist had worked in England.

Prince Charles did not, therefore, grow up among noble works of art which would have awakened and formed his taste. On the walls of his father's palaces there were no doubt some fine portraits sent as gifts by foreign potentates, and he would have seen some at least of the works of Holbein. But the tradition of the English Court for the last fifty years had been markedly indifferent to the visual arts. Sovereigns had not even valued the treasures they possessed. A beautiful little *Saint George* by Raphael, now in the National Gallery in Washington, D.C. (and reproduced in the portfolio that accompanies this article), had been given to King Henry VII by the Duke of Urbino, but one of his successors had passed it on to a favored courtier.

Charles's father, King James I, showed little interest in works of art. But the Queen, the lively and high-spirited Danish princess, Anne, made up for her husband's indifference by her own expansive tastes and her love of all the arts of adornment and display. Year after year she took part in Court masques, where painted scenery and skillful lighting set off the intricate and glittering dresses of the performers. The presiding genius of these occasions was Inigo Jones, the Italian-trained architect, designer, and draftsman. It was surely as an enthralled spectator of his mother's masques that the young Prince Charles acquired his earliest understanding of the beauty of color, form, and design.

Meanwhile, English noblemen traveling abroad were beginning to share in the prevalent European taste for collecting works of art. While Charles was growing up, the Earl of Arundel was bringing his famous "marbles" to England—classical statues, busts, sarcophagi, and inscriptions. But the most ambitious of these English noble collectors was the meteoric Duke of Buckingham. This handsome youth, the younger son of a country squire, became the favorite of King James in 1616 and for the next twelve years was the greatest man in England. Politically, his influence was disastrous; but as far as collecting works of art was concerned, he may be said to have turned England's tentative dawn into a blaze of daylight. He had a genuine taste for the beautiful, and the wealth he amassed as the King's favorite enabled him rapidly to become a collector of European fame.

The elder son of King James, Prince Henry, who died suddenly at the age of eighteen, had also developed a taste for collecting. His death made Charles, then twelve years old, not only heir to the throne but also the possessor of his brother's choice collection of rarities. These included a few books and pictures and a considerable number of coins and medals, with a group of eighteen small bronzes of Florentine workmanship. Just before his death Henry had summoned to England a Dutch craftsman, Abraham van der Doort, an expert in the detailed work that Henry liked. This excellent man, who seems to have been at one time in the service of another collector, the melancholy, mad Emperor Rudolf II, now became the devoted adviser of the young Prince Charles. He gave him, for instance, a copy of Dürer's famous book illustrating perspective, proportion, and the human form in art. Later he was appointed keeper of Charles's growing collection, which he carefully catalogued, thus leaving to future art historians the invaluable evidence on which much of our knowledge of the King's possessions is based.

By the time Prince Charles was twenty, it was beginning to be known outside England that he aspired to be a collector and patron. English diplomatic representatives in the Netherlands were already ordering pictures for him from the studio of Rubens. The giant of contemporary European painting, Rubens kept a workshop of assistants busy fulfilling, under his direction, orders received from all the princely houses of Europe. Prince Charles flattered him greatly by insisting on acquiring for himself a self-portrait, which the master, after a becomingly modest hesitation, agreed to send him. It is still today in the royal collection.

Yet Charles was not so dazzled by the name of Rubens as to accept everything that came from his studio with uncritical pleasure. A *Lion Hunt* was not approved. Far from being insulted, Rubens seems to have respected all the more a patron who would not be satisfied with anything short of the best. He was to say later that only paintings entirely from his own hand were good enough for Charles.

Thanks to Buckingham, Arundel, and a few others the

TEXT CONTINUED ON PAGE 89

On the Following Pages: A Portfolio in Gravure of Paintings from Charles I's Collection

MANTEGNA: THE DORMITION OF THE VIRGIN, C. 1462

PRADO, MADRID

TITIAN: GIRL IN A FUR WRAP, C. 1534
KUNSTHISTORISCHES MUSEUM, VIENNA

OVERLEAF
GIORGIONE: FETE CHAMPETRE, C. 1510
LOUVRE, PARIS

TITIAN: EMPEROR CHARLES V WITH A DOG, C. 1533

PRADO, MADRID

TITIAN: MADONNA WITH THE RABBIT (DETAIL), C. 1530

LOUVRE, PARIS

RAPHAEL: ST. GEORGE AND THE DRAGON, C. 1505

NATIONAL GALLERY OF ART (MELLON COLLECTION), WASHINGTON, D. C.

VAN DYCK: SELF-PORTRAIT WITH ENDYMION PORTER, C. 1633

PRADO, MADRID

TEXT CONTINUED FROM PAGE 80
number of works of art in England was steadily increasing. But even so, there were relatively few great pictures on which Charles could form his taste. Works of art familiar today to every educated person through the medium of the photograph could at that time be known only by reputation, or by description, or perhaps by an occasional copy or engraving. Charles must have studied much more carefully, and cherished much more, the beautiful things that were directly available to him; but by our standards his youthful taste was nourished on a starvation diet.

Small wonder that when, in his twenty-third year, he visited Spain, the art of the Renaissance broke upon him like a revelation. He went to Madrid with Buckingham, now his closest friend and mentor, hoping to bring back as his bride the Infanta, sister to King Philip IV. As a wooer he failed, but the visit to Spain was for him, as an art collector, the turning point of his life. He saw at Madrid and in the Escorial, paintings more plentiful and more wonderful than he had ever seen before. Here the shy, inhibited youth found the answer to his dearest desires in the glowing color of Titian, the poetic grace of Raphael, the feminine delicacy of the then much-admired Correggio. The overwhelming impact of beauty, so rich and so various, on a mind deeply receptive to impressions of visual pleasure can only be imagined.

Though he brought no wife home from Spain, Charles brought home a number of presents. King Philip gave him the splendid Titian known as the *Venus of Pardo*—a naked nymph asleep in a woodland landscape among satyrs, hunting dogs, and figures of the chase—which now hangs in the Louvre. He gave him also Titian's fine portrait of Emperor Charles V with what the English called his "high white Irish dog," and as a piquant contrast, Titian's mischievous young girl, inadequately concealing her charms in the folds of a fur wrap (both paintings are reproduced in the portfolio). Apart from these and other acquisitions, Charles had been able while in Spain to establish himself in the small world of European collectors, painters, and dealers as a potential buyer of great significance.

Within a year of his return to England, Charles succeeded his father on the throne and set about gratifying his artistic tastes to the full. The agents who looked out for works of art for him included such eminent persons as his ambassadors and representatives abroad, especially those at Venice, Brussels, Madrid, and Vienna. Throughout the peaceful years of his reign he constantly received information from them about pictures for sale, and sometimes also presents. Diplomats visiting him from other rulers knew that a piece of valuable information, or better still a gift, would smooth the way of their political negotiations. Pope Urban VIII, himself a lavish patron, was careful to send to the English Court envoys who could combine with their overtures for the King's return to the Catholic faith (which he resisted) a sensitive sympathy with his tastes.

Besides such distinguished agents and helpers, Charles also made full use of more professional go-betweens, usually artists. Like other collectors of his time he often wanted to have copies of important works that were not for sale. Some of the copyists he sent to Italy or Spain made it their task to report back to him any news of pictures for sale, or potentially for sale, that they happened to hear. It was regarded as part of their job. The most important of these agents was probably the widely gifted Nicolas Lanière: his real profession was that of musician to the King; but he was also a competent artist, and he traveled for three crucial years in Italy, from 1625 to 1628, gaining much valuable knowledge and playing a vital part in the expansion of the King's collection.

Another important but rather more dubious character was Balthasar Gerbier, miniaturist, amateur educationist, diplomat, and friend of Rubens, who combined his numerous professions with art collecting, first on behalf of Buckingham, and later on behalf of Charles; and he seems to have thrown in a little spying and betraying of state secrets on the side.

One of Charles's earliest coups was to acquire in 1623 the seven huge Raphael cartoons of the *Acts of the Apostles,* originally drawn for tapestries in the Vatican. When they reached England, he lent them to the new tapestry factory that he was encouraging near London, at Mortlake, where they were copied, sometimes with borders added from designs that have been attributed to Van Dyck. A few of these beautiful sets have survived in English country houses. Though the King's pleasure in art was deeply personal, he also had a conscious and constructive hope that by bringing important works of art to England and enabling artists to see and study them, he would stimulate the lagging talents of the English themselves and create, perhaps, native arts and native workmanship not unworthy of such great originals. His use of the Raphael cartoons was a part of this grander plan.

After the failure of his courtship of the Infanta, Charles had married Henrietta Maria, the young sister of Louis XIII of France. On her mother's side the Princess was a Medici, a family among whom love of the visual arts was a guiding tradition. The little bride had been distressed at the thought of leaving Paris to join her new husband without seeing a series of pictures by Rubens that her mother, Marie de Médicis, had recently commissioned for the Luxembourg Palace. The obliging painter did his utmost to complete them before the date fixed for her departure. When she had settled down to her new life in England, Queen Henrietta Maria joined with her husband in making their palaces beautiful, and several times he acquired works of art especially for her. He seems also to have believed in starting his children young in the way they should go, and it is on record that he gave "with his own hand" a picture described as "a little perspective piece" to his second son when he was barely five.

In 1627 King Charles made his most stupendous haul, a

purchase which vastly increased the extent of his collection and made it instantly the most important in Europe. He acquired almost the entire collection assembled by the Gonzaga Dukes of Mantua during several generations of lavish patronage and purchases. The last of the Gonzaga family, debauched and bankrupt, decided to sell. For this tremendous treasure house, which contained important works by Titian, Tintoretto, Mantegna, and Correggio, as well as those by more recent painters very much in the contemporary fashion, such as Caravaggio and Domenico Fetti, there was of course great competition. Negotiations for the sale were thus secret and complex. Cardinal Richelieu was particularly anxious to secure the prize for the honor and glory of France. But thanks to good organization, discreet approaches to the Duke, and the skill of the dealer whom he employed, one Daniel Nys, Charles carried off the great mass of the Mantuan pictures. Two years later he added to his by now massive acquisitions a series of paintings by Mantegna of the *Triumph of Julius Caesar,* which had been held back from the original Mantuan sale.

The Mantuan sale was the chance of a lifetime. In general the King acquired works of art singly or in smaller groups, though he seems to have had one remarkably big haul through an agent named William Frizell, who secured for him more than twenty Italian pictures, including several Titians, about the year 1637. More often the King enlarged his collection by one or two treasures at a time. Presents were frequently offered to him. Nuremberg sent him two pictures by its greatest painter, Albrecht Dürer. The Pope sent a bust of Charles done by Bernini, the greatest sculptor of the day, from paintings by Van Dyck. A Scottish courtier, the Earl of Ancram, himself a connoisseur of some discrimination, brought back from the Low Countries three pictures by the then young and fashionable Rembrandt as an offering to the King. When he could not buy, the King sometimes found he could exchange pictures with other collectors. He gave a Holbein portrait to his brother-in-law, Louis XIII of France, in exchange for the darkly mysterious head of Saint John the Baptist by Leonardo da Vinci. He also exchanged a volume of Holbein drawings with the Earl of Pembroke, getting in return *Saint George and the Dragon* by Raphael, which Henry VII had once owned and which had carelessly been given away.

In the meantime he continued to buy the works of distinguished contemporaries and to invite them to his Court. Of the moderns he acquired examples of Guido Reni, Simon Vouet, Orazio Gentileschi, and Gerard van Honthorst, who was the most famous of the Dutch followers of Caravaggio and who painted the charming allegory of the Liberal Arts which decorates the Queen's staircase at Hampton Court.

Charles did not stop short at commissioning pictures. He had numerous building plans, few of which came to completion. Inigo Jones, who had built the new Banqueting House at Whitehall, also built for the Queen the engaging little

All that survives today of Whitehall Palace, where Charles I lived,

white palace, still standing at Greenwich, called the Queen's House. For this, Gentileschi did a number of decorations and others were ordered from Jacob Jordaens. Charles also brought to England the French sculptor Hubert Le Sueur to make sculptural adornments to his new buildings. The artist's most famous work is the dapper little equestrian statue of King Charles which now rides, in the midst of traffic, at the northern end of Whitehall.

Charles had begun his rule by involving himself in wars with both France and Spain; but war was far more expensive than collecting pictures, and it soon became a luxury he could not afford. After the murder of his friend the bellicose Duke of Buckingham, Charles only wanted to make peace. In 1629 the Governess of the Spanish Netherlands, the Archduchess Isabella, patroness of Rubens, decided to send over no less an envoy than the great painter himself to discuss preliminary peace terms with King Charles. She could not have made a better choice. Charles welcomed him with joy, and when not discussing politics, they spent happy hours on artistic projects. It was during this visit that Rubens made final arrangements for decorating the ceiling of the new Banqueting House: the huge canvases would be done in his Antwerp studio and fixed in place when the building was completed. Rubens also restored several damaged pictures in the King's collection and copied others. He was amazed at the number of works of art that were now to be found in

RADIO TIMES HULTON PICTURE LIBRARY

...s the classical Banqueting House that Inigo Jones designed for him

England—more were there, he thought, than anywhere outside Italy. Thanks to the Earl of Arundel, the Duke of Buckingham, and above all to the King himself, England had been changed in the space of about fifteen years from a country almost barren of artistic treasures into one that, according to Rubens, every serious artist and connoisseur should make haste to visit.

While in England Rubens painted at least two important original works. As a charming compliment to the King he painted an imaginative landscape reminiscent of the Thames Valley, in which Saint George, with features somewhat resembling those of King Charles, gallantly rescues a princess who has the lively expression of Queen Henrietta Maria. When he departed, having successfully accomplished his peacemaking mission, Rubens also left behind the large joyous allegory called *Peace and War,* which hangs today in the National Gallery in London.

Five years after Rubens's departure, his paintings for the ceiling of the Banqueting House arrived and were hoisted into place. King Charles valued these radiant pictures so highly that he forbade the use of candles in the hall for fear of damage to them. This was an inconvenient prohibition because it meant, of course, that all banquets in the future would have to take place by daylight, and a new hall had to be hastily run up for any functions held after dark. In spite of his pleasure in the new ceiling the King took more than three years to pay the three thousand pounds that he owed for them; he sweetened the delay—which Rubens philosophically accepted as a matter of course when dealing with royalty—by adding a gold chain as a personal gift.

In the interval between the departure of Rubens from London and the arrival of his pictures for the Banqueting House, King Charles had found the perfect court painter. Anthony Van Dyck was a generation younger than Rubens, had once worked with him, and was greatly admired by him. He had briefly visited England when Charles, as Prince of Wales, was taking his first steps as a patron, but he had not then felt tempted to stay. He had gone to Italy and in Genoa had perfected, in his portraits of the nobility, a rich Italianate style with a certain fluid, poetic quality of his own. Coming back to the Netherlands, he worked for a time in Antwerp before crossing again to England in 1632. From then until his death in 1641 he was the King's most favored painter. Charles conferred on him the honor of knighthood—which he had also conferred on Rubens—and found him a wife among the Scottish nobility.

Van Dyck made many friends in England. Among them was Endymion Porter, an art patron and collector of some distinction himself, and a man of great influence with the King, whom he served in the capacity of Gentleman of the Bedchamber. To show his gratitude and admiration for Porter, Van Dyck painted him in a double portrait with himself that now hangs in the Prado and is reproduced on the last page of the portfolio.

In England Van Dyck developed a style more gentle and pastoral than his Italian manner. His color schemes grew softer and more subtle, with iridescent grays and blues, pale amber, coral pink, and willow green—colors which seem to reflect the misty skies and half-tone weather of England. He also developed a form of outdoor portrait, setting the lords and ladies of King Charles's Court against wind-streaked skies or the trees and ornamental rocks of an English park. His portraits very beautifully interpret the escapist spirit and aesthetic conventions of the Court of King Charles I, a king who, all unknowing of the future, once called himself "the happiest King in Christendom." The Venetian ambassador, who should have been a judge of such matters, described the Court as *"la piu sontuosa e la piu allegra del mondo"*—the most sumptuous and the most joyful in the world.

The King contemplated his pictures and explained their beauties to his especial friends; he went out to gather flowers on May Day with his Queen and children; he danced with her in Court masques, both of them attired in delightful fancy dress designed by Inigo Jones; at least three times a week he went hunting—it was his favorite sport—with a band of elegant courtiers in one of his huge deer parks. He really cared very little for politics, and his ministers found it difficult to persuade him to listen to any reports of what went on in his realm unless they were cheerful and satisfactory. Foreign ambassadors knew more of what was going on in the country than the King did; Rubens had noticed that the Puritans, whom he thought were the majority of the King's subjects, were in a state of near-rebellion, and one of the Venetian envoys commented in his despatches on the mounting discontent of the people and the King's ignorance of it.

Outside the charmed circle that King Charles had made for himself, discontent grew. The King needed money, and the merchants were irritated when he put up the customs rates without recourse to Parliament. The gentry were moved to resistance when, still without calling Parliament, he extended the tax known as ship money from the seaboard counties to the inland counties. In justice to him it should be said that the money raised by this tax was scrupulously devoted to improving the Navy and not to the King's private expenses. But that did not affect the principle of non-Parliamentary taxation, and when John Hampden was prosecuted for refusing to pay, the King's own judges were not unanimous in defending the legality of the tax. All the time there was a bitter, angry muttering, in London, in the seaport towns, up and down the country, against the King's open favors to Roman Catholics and his pusillanimous foreign policy, which was making England subservient to the hereditary enemy, Spain.

Above all, the King's Puritan subjects, who were many in number and strong in character, were goaded into righteous wrath by his mistaken attempt to compel them to submit to the Anglican ritual. They disapproved of the elaborate music he had introduced into his own chapel; they were shocked at his encouragement of stage plays and appalled when they heard that the Queen herself acted in masques at Court. When William Prynne wrote a vituperative book about this, the King's Court of the Star Chamber sentenced him to have his ears cut off and to be imprisoned for life.

The Puritans objected on religious grounds to all representations of God as being opposed to the Commandments, and to all pictures of saints as idolatrous. They objected on moral grounds to anything "lascivious." It seems therefore, at first sight, odd that they raised no protests against the King's collection of pictures, which contained numerous Holy Families and pictures of saints, as well as many naked nymphs and goddesses. But the answer is simple. The royal collection was not criticized because the Puritans knew little or nothing about it. Artists and people interested in painting could usually get permission to visit the King's pictures, but these formed only a minute fraction of the public. In general the King's subjects cared too little for the visual arts to take any notice of the King's collection. They had other and more urgent matters on which to nourish their discontent.

So King Charles lived for nearly ten years in a sort of royal paradise that was also a fool's paradise. And Anthony Van Dyck was the interpreter of this lovely, doomed society. His portraits have done more than the writing of devoted Royalists to fix in the eyes of posterity the characteristics of the King and of those handsome young aristocrats, with their shining lovelocks, their Brussels lace, their glistening silks and glowing velvets, who were so soon to die in battle for their King. Above all he created for us an image of the sad-eyed monarch who came to a tragic end. Yet Van Dyck, who died some months before the Civil War broke out, had no foreknowledge of what lay ahead. The melancholy and sentimental aura which hangs about his portraits of the King is largely the effect of imagination. But if we can bring ourselves to look at these famous portraits objectively, they reveal with uncanny clearness the art of the court painter at its highest. Van Dyck gave the King an air of aloof and pensive dignity which is wholly missing from the portraits of him by other painters. Yet he did not flatter him. The face as he painted it is not handsome: the nose is too large, the features irregular, the mouth rather loose, the eyes often rimmed with red. But we hardly notice these things because Van Dyck subtly concentrates our attention on the fine forehead and the lofty expression of the whole face. He shows us a man of noble thoughts, posed with quiet dignity. Because he is careful never to paint the King at all close to anyone else—except occasionally the Queen—we do not realize that this commanding figure measured a bare five feet. His Queen, happily for him, was even smaller.

The first dark shadow fell across the peaceful years of Charles's reign in 1638 when his subjects in Scotland revolted against his religious policy, provoking sympathetic resistance among all the English Puritans. Though the King's income had sufficed for his expensive tastes in the arts—largely thanks to the ingenuity of his finance ministers—it was far too small to enable him to raise the necessary forces to restore order and enforce his authority. Nemesis had come: he had to call Parliament. The gentry, merchants, and lawyers in Parliament cared nothing at all for his buildings, his collections, or his encouragement of the arts; but they cared very much about his repression of the Puritans, his dubious taxation measures, and his coquetting with the leading Roman Catholic powers in Europe. The unhappy King found his ministers arrested and his powers curtailed; and by 1642 he had to flee from his capital, leaving all his great collections behind him. For the next four years, in the course of a long civil war in which he strove unsuccessfully to reaffirm his power, he had neither time nor money to give to the arts. But there is a sort of pathos in his faint attempts to maintain something of his old standards in the turmoil of war. In his military headquarters at Oxford he employed William Dobson, the only really talented English painter before the eighteenth century. Dobson had studied the Italian pictures in the royal collection in the happy days of peace, and he modeled his style in portraiture ambitiously on Tintoretto; at best he can be darkly impressive, as some of his wartime pictures of the King's loyal generals show.

BY PERMISSION OF THE TRUSTEES OF THE BRITISH MUSEUM

The ups and downs of royal fortunes are illustrated by an engraving in which Pierre Lombart in about 1658 copied the body and horse of Van Dyck's equestrian portrait of Charles I, but substituted (left) the head of Cromwell, then Lord Protector. After the Restoration Lombart removed Cromwell's head (center) and later replaced it with that of Charles (right).

Later, as a prisoner in the hands of Parliament, Charles lived for a time at his own palace of Hampton Court, where he could at least enjoy some of his pictures while negotiating with Cromwell. Perhaps it was in these months that Cromwell acquired a certain knowledge of, and respect for, fine painting. He was not to show himself without taste when he became Lord Protector, and it seems likely that the King could not resist the pleasure of showing and explaining to him some of his treasures. Charles, at this time, made one last venture in patronage, having his portrait painted by a young Dutchman named Peter Lely who had recently come to England. But after an abortive attempt to escape, his fortunes dipped steeply. Even during his last close imprisonment, while his trial was pending, he seems to have spent some time in poring over architectural plans for the enlargement of Whitehall. Perhaps it was no more than an attempt to escape from the reality of the moment into what he now knew to be no more than a dream. His portrait was painted once again, but he cannot have been aware of the fact when he gave his last sitting. It was during his trial. A pedestrian limner named Edward Bower made rapid sketches from which he later worked up several portraits to sell to devoted Royalists. In this last known picture the King is pale, haggard, and heavily bearded, but is still recognizable as the dignified monarch whom Van Dyck had painted in his glory. He was executed on January 30, 1649.

A few weeks afterward the Council of State of the young English republic decided to sell the King's goods in order to pay debts that he had contracted in his lifetime. In view of other and more dreadful possibilities, lovers of art ought perhaps to be grateful for the decision. During the English Civil War, as at all times of public disorder, a terrible lust for destruction had swept the country. Apart from a few fanatics, educated Puritans objected to works of art only when they were set up for worship in churches or otherwise exhibited in a way that could corrupt religion or morals. It was not educated Puritans who wrought most of the destruction but mobs of soldiers and seamen whom their leaders could not control. They sacked cathedrals and occasionally country mansions, smashing the painted glass and the statues, burning the hangings, illuminated manuscripts, and paintings. The Queen's chapel, with an altarpiece by Rubens, was sacked early in the war; but Parliament took charge of the King's various palaces and preserved them against violence.

The extent of the King's collection was now realized, and some who saw it disapproved of it. One dour fanatic in Parliament seems to have called for the destruction of everything idolatrous and lascivious in it. But most members of Parliament were aware at least of the potential value of the pictures; some also recognized their prestige value and their usefulness as impressive decorations for those parts of the royal palaces that they were already using for government offices or for entertaining distinguished foreign visitors.

So it happened that the collection was still intact at the King's death when the English republic, hard-pressed for money, took the decision to sell. Cromwell has sometimes been credited with holding back some of the best pieces for use in the palaces which were shortly to become his. But although he was often at this time chairman of the Council of State, the decisions seem to have been taken jointly, and in any case he was away campaigning in Ireland and Scotland when most of the sales took place. They began in the spring of 1649, and the business was not well managed. The pictures, running to nearly fourteen hundred, were given approximate values, and a reserve price was put on some of them. The government of the newly formed republic had decided to hold back a maximum of twenty thousand pounds worth of the King's goods (including jewelry, furniture, and hangings—so there was not much balance for pictures) for its own use. The Raphael cartoons might still be useful to the state for the manufacture of tapestry; and Mantegna's splendid *Triumph of Julius Caesar* was especially suitable for the walls of an official building. As a result both these important groups of pictures remained in the royal collection.

After the initial sale, where the Spanish ambassador bought lavishly for his master King Philip IV, the matter seems to have dragged on. Pictures were still being sold as late as 1657. Lesser works of art were grouped together in lots and, to save trouble, were sometimes allotted in lieu of cash to the creditors of the late King. A few buyers in England came forward out of genuine loyalty to rescue the royal treasures. Among them one finds names familiar in earlier years when the collection was being assembled: Nicolas Lanière, for instance, came forward as a buyer and also Emmanuel De Critz, another painter and copyist who had worked for Charles in the old days. After his restoration to the throne in 1660, Charles II was able to recover some of his father's possessions from these exceptional buyers and from some of those who had taken pictures to settle debts. In this way he got back, for example, the two magnificent Tintoretto canvases which are today in the royal collection: *The Nine Muses,* a sunlit pattern of air-borne goddesses in a summer sky, and his nobly pathetic picture of Esther before Ahasuerus.

The greater number of the masterpieces were sold to foreign rulers. The King of Spain, Cardinal Mazarin, Queen Christina of Sweden, and the Archduke Leopold Wilhelm, Governor of the Spanish Netherlands, were among the principal buyers. One faithful Royalist, the Earl of Clarendon, who later wrote his famous *History of the Rebellion,* was in Spain on a mission from the despised and exiled Prince of Wales, soon to be Charles II, when no less than eighteen cartloads of the dismembered collection of the dead King came trundling into Madrid.

The prices realized were undoubtedly a disappointment to the English government. They had hoped for about £200,000 (say about six million dollars in modern money), and they raised little more than £50,000. Not knowing very much about selling works of art, and not being well advised, they seem to have made the initial mistake of throwing all the pictures at once onto a market already flooded. The disordered years of the Civil War had caused ruined Royalist families to sell some of their possessions, and on two or three occasions the contents of some huge mansion had been auctioned by the victorious Parliamentary troops immediately after its capture. The collection of the Duke of Buckingham, second only to that of the King, had been put up for sale by his descendants only a few months before the King's own came up.

The individual prices paid for the King's pictures are an interesting index to the relative esteem in which painters were then held. The highest paid was £2,000 for the exquisite little Raphael Madonna known as *"La Perla,"* now in the Prado. The next highest was £1,000 for the Correggio *Sleeping Antiope,* now in the Louvre; Correggio was not only very fashionable, but his paintings, outside his native Parma, were comparatively rare. Titian, though he was regarded with great respect, had been a prolific painter, and his work was fairly often on the market. Even so, £600 seems a small sum to have paid for the sumptuous *Venus of Pardo,* now in the Louvre. The King of Spain bought back for a mere £150 Titian's full-length portrait of the Emperor Charles V with his dog. Another surprisingly low price was £140 for Leonardo da Vinci's *Saint John the Baptist,* though the picture was in poor condition, and the raised arm of the saint was described in Van der Doort's catalogue as being "wronged by some washing"—an early reference to the deleterious effect of careless cleaning. Acquired by Cardinal Mazarin, it passed a few years later to Louis XIV.

The greater number of the pictures which had been the pride and joy of King Charles were thus dispersed. Of the few that remained in the royal collection or found their way back to it, the most important besides the two Tintorettos are Giorgione's beautiful head of a shepherd boy, a Correggio *Holy Family* and a *Saint Catherine,* a *Lucretia* by Titian, the self-portrait by Rubens that had been one of the King's earliest acquisitions, and a Rembrandt portrait of the artist's mother. A fair number of lesser pictures also remained unsold or came back to the King's descendants, but it was a mere wreck of the great collection that had been. Not until George IV, as Prince Regent, set himself up as patron and collector did any English monarch again begin to build a royal collection on an ambitious scale.

A few of the King's pictures later found their way back to England when, in the nineteenth century, economic and political change again broke up some of the great private collections of Europe. Among these was the enchanting Correggio *Education of Cupid* and Dürer's fine portrait of his father, both now in the National Gallery in London. But many more have remained scattered far and wide abroad. The Prado contains, among others, Raphael's *"La Perla";*

Titian's *Saint Margaret,* his portrait of Emperor Charles V with his dog, *The Marquis del Guasto Addressing His Troops, Venus with the Organ-player;* Veronese's *Marriage at Cana;* a *Holy Family* by Andrea del Sarto; a self-portrait by Dürer; and the serenely beautiful *Dormition of the Virgin* by Mantegna (reproduced on the first page of the portfolio), with its nobly grouped figures and luminous view of Mantua beyond the arches which frame the scene. This great picture had been one of the many treasures which Charles had bought from the bankrupt Mantuan Duke. At Vienna, which they reached by way of the collection of the Archduke Leopold Wilhelm, are Titian's *Girl in a Fur Wrap*—the treasure that Charles had carried home from Spain as a youth of twenty-three—and Parmigianino's *Saint Catherine,* along with several Van Dycks. Mantegna's austerely foreshortened *Dead Christ* is now in the Brera at Milan, and Raphael's far-traveled *Saint George and the Dragon* ultimately reached Washington after spending a century and a half in the Hermitage Gallery at St. Petersburg, for which it was bought by Catherine the Great.

But the greatest number still to be seen together are in the Louvre, which they reached for the most part by way of Cardinal Mazarin's purchases. They include Leonardo da Vinci's *Saint John the Baptist,* Holbein's *Portrait of Erasmus,* Caravaggio's huge *Death of the Virgin,* a Correggio *Holy Family,* the wonderful *Fête Champêtre* attributed to Giorgione (reproduced in the portfolio), and an array of Titians—*The Entombment;* the *Venus of Pardo; Christ at Emmaus;* the *Girl Doing Her Hair;* the lovely *Allegory of Alfonso d'Avalos,* with its luminous center of a great crystal globe; the *Man with a Glove;* and the delightful *Madonna with the Rabbit* (see portfolio). Add to this a great number of Van Dycks, which include the finest portrait ever painted of Charles himself, the famous *Roi à la chasse* (page 78). In the same room hang Van Dyck portraits of the King's nephew Prince Rupert, looking at fifteen a gentle, dreamy adolescent whose sensitive face seems unsuited to the military suit of armor in which he is dressed and, nearby, the fair-haired Duke of Richmond, the King's cousin. All date from the time before the monarch's troubles began. The day would come when the "happiest King in Christendom" would go down in bloodshed, when the sensitive Prince Rupert would become the fiercest soldier in his uncle's cause, and when poor easygoing Richmond would vainly offer to take the King's place on the scaffold. His offer being rejected, he with three other loyalists, would bear his master's coffin to an obscure grave through the falling snow and trace on the lid no other epitaph than the words: "King Charles 1649."

Among Miss Wedgwood's recent books as a leading historian of the seventeenth century are The King's Peace *and* The King's War. *To the first issue of* HORIZON *(September, 1958) she contributed "The Golden Age of the Dutch Republic."*

RADIO TIMES HULTON PICTURE LIBRARY

Charles I made his final exit from a window of the Banqueting House, through which he stepped directly onto the scaffold

On Stage: ANNA MOFFO

In the wardrobe of Anna Moffo, the American soprano who, in 1959, became at twenty-four the youngest Violetta to make her debut at the Metropolitan Opera and who has since become one of the principal adornments of the house, are 120 hats, 75 pairs of shoes—and three sweaters emblazoned with the athletic letters of the Radnor (Pa.) High School. As a class, sopranos are not given to collecting athletic letters, but then Miss Moffo (who won gold trophies for basketball, tennis, and hockey) is not an easily classified soprano. Even before she started to study voice formally, she declined a proffered Hollywood contract, thus surmounting a temptation which operatic sopranos almost never have to overcome. And after she had brushed up on her vocal technique and embarked for further study in Italy, she was still not convinced that singing was her career: "I decided," she says, "to see Europe before I got behind the typewriter."

Miss Moffo, of course, never had any real intention of becoming a secretary, no matter how firmly she insists on that near-folly of her youth. Her voice, as it happens, was always too promising for that. Essentially lyric in quality, it has—particularly in the upper registers—all the agility and virtuosity necessary for the negotiation of coloratura scales and trills. To the soaring ease of Miss Moffo's more perilous vocal flights is added a velvety lower register and a generally immaculate sense of phrasing. Furthermore, she knows how to act with her voice—a talent more often talked about than observed on the operatic stage. And no soprano now singing is better equipped physically to suggest that she is tearing a lovesick tenor's passion to tatters. (Miss Moffo, who now makes her home in Italy with her husband, Mario Lanfranchi, and who is known there as "L'Esòtica," has been voted one of that country's "ten most beautiful women.") This amalgam of vocal and dramatic qualities enabled "the exotic" from Pennsylvania—fetchingly got up in a blonde wig—to score a notable triumph last winter at the Metropolitan as Gilda in *Rigoletto* and to unfurl an ecstatic "Caro nome" that few who were present are likely to forget. Miss Moffo, it became apparent, belongs to that company of sopranos—Birgit Nilsson, Leontyne Price, Joan Sutherland—whose joint talents constitute an emergent golden age of song.

Miss Moffo's affinity for opera and the Italian cultural climate is partially inherited: her father, who owns a shoe-repair shop in Wayne, Pennsylvania, is descended from a family that flourished in the wine-and-olive-producing region of the Abruzzi in central Italy, an area that can also take genetic credit for the voices of Mario Lanza and Perry Como. As a girl, Miss Moffo was already singing in the school choir, in recitals, at weddings and funerals. But it was not until after she had graduated from high school and entered the Curtis Institute in Philadelphia on a scholarship, that she began to get serious vocal training. Miss Moffo applied herself to her vocal studies with such success that she was asked to remain an extra year and to appear with the Philadelphia Orchestra. In what she regards as the most important decision of her career, she decided instead to accept a Fulbright scholarship for study in Italy.

It was not so much her voice that immediately impressed the Italians, Miss Moffo thinks, but her ability to sight-read, a talent that few Italian singers bother to cultivate. A few days after she reached Italy, in 1954, she was engaged to substitute, in a recital at Venice, for Elisabeth Schwarzkopf, who had been taken ill. A year later she stepped onto an operatic stage for the first time in a Spoleto production of *Don Pasquale*. Anna Moffo became "L'Esòtica" only after appearing in an Italian television production of *Madame Butterfly* in 1956, a role that she secured over the objections of the producer (he thought that at five-foot-seven she was too tall). During their discussions of Cio-Cio-San, the producer—Signor Lanfranchi—and Miss Moffo became engaged.

Impatient with some of the more blatant dramatic absurdities of the traditional operatic stage, Miss Moffo dismisses them as "ridiculous for our time. Audiences will no longer tolerate the old static performances. I study the libretto first, then the music, trying to make the dramatic part acceptable." This freshness of view has led her to re-examine the historical assumptions of any role she undertakes. "For me," she says, "opera is history."

Miss Moffo's appetite for study, abetted by her intelligence and superior memory, has resulted in an astonishing repertory of eighty roles; she has performed more than fifty. Her favorites are the leads in *La Traviata, Lucia di Lammermoor, I Puritani,* and *Manon.* (So fine, and dramatically effective, is Miss Moffo's Violetta in *Traviata*, that the Metropolitan acceded to demand and sent the production on this spring's tour, although it was not in the past season's repertory.) Her interest in acting has led her into straight dramatic roles in films; in the forthcoming *Austerlitz*, starring Orson Welles, she plays a mistress of Napoleon.

Miss Moffo possesses a strong sense of operatic mission. When she was sixteen, the singer recalls, she "suffered a religious crisis" and almost became a nun. "But the priest was very wise," she says. "He advised me not to waste the gift God had given me. He told me to take the score rather than the veil."

RICHARD MURPHY

Photograph by EUGENE COOK

On Stage: STEPHEN SONDHEIM

There is an engaging song in *West Side Story* in which the young heroine, Maria, blurts out the joy of being in love:

> *I feel pretty, oh, so pretty,*
> *That the city should give me its key.*
> *A committee*
> *Should be organized to honor me. . . .*

Besides being pleasant, the lyric is a model of craftsmanship. It states a simple emotion, clearly and with precision, and yet it is not dry. It has a girlish lilt, a touch of humor, and, as all good lyrics should, an element of surprise—in this case a triple, mainly internal rhyme.

Nevertheless the man who wrote it, Stephen Sondheim, wanted to remove the song from *West Side Story* during its tryout. He felt that the lyric, though technically expert, was wrong for Maria: she would not use a three-syllable word or express herself in such a complex pattern. Sondheim was overruled by his three collaborators, composer Leonard Bernstein, writer Arthur Laurents, and director-choreographer Jerome Robbins; but he still broods over the fact that the song gives the show a false moment.

Sondheim's reaction illustrates the particular nature of his talent—a talent of first magnitude, for at thirty-one he has already written the lyrics to two of the most robust and admired hits of the contemporary musical theater, the other being *Gypsy* (1959). If he were merely a brilliant technician, the two shows would not have made such an impact. It is because his lyrics so surely fit not only the moment but the total mood and character of the story that *West Side Story* and *Gypsy* have an extra unity, maturity, and dramatic strength. Thus when, early in *Gypsy*, Rose announces in an acrid song that it's all right for "some people" to go on "living life in a living room," but not for *her*, the audience knows that cold ambition is to be the goad for all that follows; and every lyric that she sings thereafter reveals some facet of the same hard personality. "Those are the lyrics," Sondheim says, "that come easiest—ones that deal with bitter, driving, hostile, and ambitious people."

Such an affinity might suggest that Sondheim himself is all these things. Actually the description which once might have been applied to him has almost ceased to fit him now that he has crossed into his mellow thirties and onto the sweet shores of success. But some people still find Sondheim gloomy. "Steve has a compulsion not to enjoy himself," one of his close friends says, though in company he is relatively cheerful. He has a wry and facile wit, which is reflected in many of his lyrics, such as the sardonic "Gee, Officer Krupke!" of *West Side Story*.

Sondheim prizes solitude and can happily spend days alone in his town house in the Turtle Bay section of Manhattan—a house which the editor Maxwell Perkins once owned (and which has the further cachet of being next door to Katharine Hepburn). There he indulges his addiction, which shows all signs of being incurable, to puzzles and games. In fact, he has invented a number of games that have their own gaudy boards, cards, score pads, and other utensils. One of them, "Hal Prince," named for the thriving Broadway producer, covers the full cycle of play production from selecting a script to coaxing it through a long run. Sondheim geared his game, which takes at least four hours, to the economics of the New York theater and proudly points out that it has never been won by anybody but Hal Prince.

He enjoys puzzles for their restrictions. This is providential, for one of the most restrictive of all puzzles is the 32-bar song, and he views lyrics mainly as a problem demanding, almost defying, solution. "It's not an art but a craft," says Sondheim, who imposes strict rules on himself. "I really don't like to write lyrics." What he *does* like to write is music, being a composer by training, and from now on he will at least set his hard-wrought lyrics to his own melodies. (His musical based on the comedies of Plautus is due soon; he has also written the incidental music to two recent plays.) By instinct a musical romantic who likes Brahms and Ravel, by education a modernist who likes Stravinsky and Prokofiev even better, Sondheim falls between the two schools in his own composing, which is dissonant in harmonic structure and quite pure in melody.

After Williams College, Sondheim studied composition in New York for three years. When Lemuel Ayers commissioned him to write the music and lyrics to *Saturday Night* in 1954, his prospects suddenly soared. They sank just as suddenly when, score finished and money half raised, Ayers died. (Sondheim meanwhile raised money for himself by writing *Topper* TV scripts.) But in the fall of 1955 came the golden chance to write the lyrics of *West Side Story,* and *Gypsy* came tumbling after.

A New Yorker born, bred, and so rooted that he can hardly be persuaded to leave Manhattan for the afternoon, Sondheim confesses that he is "parochial" about his city and "wouldn't be able to handle" a subject as rural as *Carousel* or as exotic as *The King and I.* This would seem to be the only visible limit to his future. Right now, as he has written in another connection, everything is coming up roses.

WILLIAM K. ZINSSER

Photograph by HANS NAMUTH

Emily Dickinson's love poems are

among the greatest she wrote,

but to whom did she address them?

Here is a new theory

"The Errand from My Heart–"

Emily Dickinson

Three of Emily Dickinson's four important biographers are agreed as to the identity of the gentleman about whom she wrote her anguished poems of love and renunciation. Thomas H. Johnson and Richard Chase and the late George F. Whicher have all accepted the theory that the man was the Rev. Charles Wadsworth of Philadelphia. Coming after years of others' wild, untenable theorizings, and coming as it does from excellent scholars, this agreement ought to be a relief all around—if true.

Millicent Todd Bingham, the other of these four and now the closest living tie with the Dickinson family, has published the documents of Emily's love in her last years for Judge Otis P. Lord of Salem, Massachusetts; but Mrs. Bingham has carefully endorsed no nominee for the one love in Emily's life important to our curiosity since it was a source of American literature. Closeness to the family warrants no special validation, in view of the publications of Martha Bianchi, Emily's niece: her self-contradictory innuendoes on this very point demonstrate that literally she did not know what she was talking about. However, Mrs. Bingham always knows what she is talking about, and her caution is as impressive as her colleagues' agreement. Not without caution (for what is circumstantial evidence that we should be mindful only of it?) I suggest that the man was Samuel Bowles.

All readers of Emily Dickinson biographies know about Samuel Bowles, the editor of the Springfield *Republican*. He has been prominent all the while, cast in the role of one of Emily's great friends and even as her especial "confidant." True, her published letters to Bowles contain some passionately worshipful remarks, but these have been gently estimated as part and parcel of Emily's exaggerated oddities; and meanwhile there has been the absorbing strain of anointing the Rev. Mr. Wadsworth to the point of "assuming" he "must have" visited Emily in Amherst in 1861—there is no evidence at all that he did—and by giving her advance news that he was moving his pastorate from Philadelphia (quite far in those days from Amherst) to San Francisco (admittedly, somewhat farther) precipitated a tremendous crisis in her life and work which occurred 1861–1862. There is a mass of evidence as to the crisis and none whatsoever that Charles Wadsworth caused it; none whatsoever as to the in-

By WINFIELD TOWNLEY SCOTT

dividual who caused it—unless we decide that all this while Samuel Bowles has been miscast. Guesswork is inevitable—I have eminent precedents there; but in addition, a new correlation and a new reading of materials seems wholly to support what has to begin as an *a priori* hunch that only Bowles fits all the requirements of dates, narrative, character, and the general situation.

Let us see, for the while without argument, how the story runs.

Apparently Emily Dickinson and Samuel Bowles first met on 11 August, 1859, a Commencement Day at Amherst College. Bowles was thirty-three years old and Emily was going on twenty-nine. For the past eight years Bowles had been editing the Springfield *Republican*, inherited from his father. He edited with a strenuous brilliance which had given the paper and himself a national reputation. The Dickinsons always read the *Republican*, and of the meager seven poems of Emily's which appeared during her lifetime (out of a retrieved 1,775 poems) five were published in that newspaper.

Bearded, strong-eyed, handsome, Samuel Bowles at thirty-three was a distinguished young man both in his looks and his achievement. He was married—very much so: in all, his wife, Mary, bore him ten children. Mrs. Bowles was with him on that first visit to the Dickinsons, and immediately afterward Emily began writing warm and affectionate letters to them. She several times apologized for writing so frequently.

Mr. and Mrs. Bowles visited again in Amherst in the summer of 1861. Again that fall, during a stay in Northampton for some sort of water cure, Bowles came over alone. That time, Emily avoided seeing him but she wrote him at once. Thereafter most of her letters—all the interesting ones—are addressed to Bowles, often with a dutiful "Love for Mary" appended. In any case, nobody has ever suggested it was *Mrs.* Bowles for whom Emily felt such special adulation. "Poor Emily! She is her own worst enemy," Mrs. Bowles reportedly remarked.

Bowles was overworked and ill that fall—seriously enough so that the following April he was to go abroad alone for his health, and Emily, the same month, was to say in the second of her letters to Thomas Wentworth Higginson that she had "a terror since September, I could tell to none; and so I sing, as the boy does by the burying ground, because I am afraid." During the intervening winter Bowles and his family lived in New York, probably because Bowles was having medical treatment there. Emily's letters to him all winter and spring grieve over his bad health. She herself felt "very ill." Early in the year she wrote Samuel Bowles:

"You spoke of the 'East.' I have thought about it this winter.

"Don't you think you and I should be shrewder to take the mountain road?

"That bareheaded life, under the grass, worries one like a wasp."

A son had been born to the Bowleses in December in New York, and Emily begged them to name him Robert, in honor of Robert Browning whose famous wife had died earlier that year. Emily's admiration for Elizabeth Barrett Browning was huge. "Will you call him Robert for me? He is the bravest man alive, but *his* boy has no mamma." And, next month, "—did you vote upon 'Robert'?" What is of prime interest here is not the literary reference but Emily's strange rushing-in, a gratuitous insistence unexplainable except as vicarious participation. Seen thus, a touching revelation. The child was named Charles. Even the following summer Emily, writing to Mrs. Bowles, inquires for "Robert."

In March, 1862, Bowles again appeared in Amherst, apparently with Mrs. Bowles. Emily avoided a meeting and immediately wrote him: "Perhaps you thought I didn't care—because I stayed out, yesterday. I *did* care, Mr. Bowles. I pray for your sweet health to Allah every morning, but something troubled me, and I knew you needed light and air, so I didn't come. Nor have I the conceit that you *noticed* me. . . . It grieves me till I cannot speak, that you are suffering."

One is reminded of a poem Emily wrote, perhaps a year or two before this, beginning "I should not dare to leave my friend," and expressing the fear of death. Its second stanza:

If I should disappoint the eyes
That hunted—hunted so—to see—
And could not bear to shut until
They "noticed" me—they noticed me—

The Rev. Charles Wadsworth

On the 5th of April, Samuel Bowles returned to Amherst to say goodbye to the Dickinsons. From the tone of her anticipatory letters, Emily intended to see him on that important occasion, and we may well believe she did see him. On the 9th he sailed from New York. On the 15th Emily wrote her first letter to Higginson, which was in its way her first letter to the world: to ask "if my verse is alive?" On the 25th, in another letter, she referred to her "terror since September." She was sick abed as she wrote.

Now we come to the "Daisy" letters. There are three of them. They are in Emily's handwriting of the early 1860's. They address a "Master," and Emily refers to herself as "Daisy." The reader will find them in Chapter XXXII of Mrs. Bingham's *Emily Dickinson's Home* where they were first published, 1955.* Mrs. Bingham leaves them up in the air of questions: to Wadsworth? Bowles? some man we know nothing of? or even—but no!—Higginson?

They are written in a style so elliptical it borders insanity. This is not unusual in Emily's correspondence: her cryptics are customarily so unexplained as to seem irrational. But the prostrate infatuation of these letters is unique in her correspondence until, late in life, her letters to Judge Lord. As with those, there is no proof these were actually mailed. It is no matter to the main point. She wrote them, and the internal evidence suggests that she wrote them to Samuel Bowles during the winter and spring of 1861–1862.

Boiled down, what information do they give us?

The first letter: Emily is in love, and hopelessly so save as she has some hope of old age with this "Master" or, barring even that, of being with him in heaven. He is not at present in New England, but would he come next summer to Amherst? He has a beard.

The second letter: They have had—for Emily—an "awful parting." Quite evidently her love is not returned: "but punish—do not banish her . . . only pledge that you will forgive . . ." etc.

The third letter: Emily is ill, but the man more so. He is somewhere at sea. And it is ("the violets are by my side") April or May in Amherst.

Among the many poems Mr. Johnson dates "about 1862" in his great edition of Dickinson, the one to note here is

The Himmaleh was known to stoop
Unto the Daisy low—
Transported with Compassion
That such a Doll should grow
Where Tent by Tent—Her Universe
Hung out it's Flags of Snow—

They are passionate letters of self-abasement, hopelessness, and love: to a bearded, unattainable man who is ill, who is not at hand, who is journeying yet farther away by sea, with whom she has recently parted in dreadful anguish for herself yet whom she might see again in a few months. And the ultimate time is spring in—I daresay—1862. For no other man than Samuel Bowles fits, and he fits perfectly. The Rev. Mr. Wadsworth, who sailed to settle in California in May of that year, would hardly be expected to visit New England come summer; Emily had met him in 1854, and we know of no other meeting between them until the second and last in 1880; and Wadsworth's vague whiskeriness—by the way—was as nothing to Bowles's stunning plumage.

In the previous July—that is, 1861—Samuel Bowles wrote a letter afterward published in his official biography with the recipient's name deleted. Rebecca Patterson calls attention to the letter in *The Riddle of Emily Dickinson:* as she says, he wrote it during a summer when he saw Emily, and it could indeed have been written to her. Mrs. Patterson's special theory of Emily's romance is unshared by me as by most people, but it does seem tenable that Bowles's words—contrary to Mrs. Patterson's interpretation—are the words of a man to a woman whose infatuation he cannot return.

The letter says in part: "You must give if you expect to receive—give happiness, friendship, love, joy, and you will

*Also, subsequently, in Johnson's three-volume edition of Emily's *Letters*. They appear as Nos. 187, 233, 248 in Volume Two. Their ordering differs from Mrs. Bingham's. No. 187 is the letter Mrs. Bingham places third. Johnson dates it "about 1858"; dates the Bingham first (his second) "about 1861"; dates the Bingham second (his third) "about 1862?" Johnson heads all three letters "To recipient unknown" and suggests that "at present one conjectures no other [than the Rev. Charles Wadsworth] whom she might thus [as 'master'] have designated." No reasons are given for the reordering or for the spread-out dating. Despite my deep respect for Johnson's scholarship I shall, for the purpose of this little detective story, cling to Mrs. Bingham.

Judge Otis P. Lord

find them floating back to you. Sometimes you will give more than you receive. We all do that in some of our relations, but it is as true a pleasure often to give without return as life can afford us. We must not make bargains with the heart, as we would with the butcher for his meat. Our business is to give what we have to give—what we can get to give. The return we have nothing to do with. It will all come in due time—in this world or another. We shall have our dues. One will not give us what we give them—others will more than we can or do give them—and so the accounts will balance themselves. It is so with my loves and friendships—it is so with everybody's. There is no call for any of us to *humble* ourselves before each other. . . ."

This is kind and careful and arm's-length, like Whitman's famous, ingenuous letter to the ardent Mrs. Anne Gilchrist. It is a very long limb of guesswork to crawl out on, the assumption that Bowles addressed it to Emily; but given the premise of their relationship it is not so far-fetched to assume that *thus* he would have had to address her—and perhaps he did.

Returning to identifiable ground, we again come to something important which cannot be fully proved. The best Dickinson authorities believe but do not know for sure that two notes accompanying poems belong among her correspondence with Bowles, and about 1862. The first accompanies a transcript of the poem beginning

Title divine—is mine!
The Wife—without the Sign!

and ending

"My Husband"—women say—
Stroking the Melody—
Is this*—the way?*

And the note says: "*Here's*—what I had to 'tell you'—You will tell no other? Honor—is it's own pawn." The second note, prefacing a transcript of the poem "Through the strait pass of suffering— The Martyrs—even—trod. . . ." says: "Dear friend If you doubted my Snow—for a moment—you never will—again—I know—

"Because I could not say it—I fixed it in the Verse—for you to read—when your thought wavers, for such a foot as mine."

These have been offered as evidence of Bowles's position as confidant for Emily, just as Mrs. Patterson offers his mysterious letter. The messages should be read—it seems to me—as confidences wholly concerning Bowles. "Here's what I had to 'tell *you*' " and "Because I could not *say* it (to you) I fixed it in the Verse for *you* to read."

Emily's published letters to Samuel Bowles abroad are very fond. "I have the errand from my heart—I might forget to tell it. Would you please to come home?" and "I tell you, Mr. Bowles, it is a suffering, to have a sea—no care how blue—between your soul and you. . . . I've learned to read the steamer place in newspapers now. It's 'most like shaking hands with you, or more like your ringing at the door."

Again, "about 1862":

I envy Seas, whereon He rides—
I envy Spokes of Wheels
Of Chariots, that Him convey—
I envy Crooked Hills

That gaze upon His journey—
How easy All can see
What is forbidden utterly
As Heaven—unto me! . . .

Does this sound like a clergyman settling into a new pastorate—or like a man far traveling?

Yet when Bowles returned and visited Amherst in November, Emily would not see him. She sent down a note about hearing his voice and, perhaps a few days later, answered a letter from him. She wrote "Because I did not see you, Vinnie and Austin upbraided me—They did not know I gave my part that they might have the more. . . . My Heart led all the rest—I think that what we *know*—we can endure that others doubt, until their faith be riper. And so, dear friend, who knew me, I make no argument—to you—

"Did I not want to see you? Do not the Phebes want to come? . . ."

How can we read this other than the act and words of a woman involved in a forbidden love, who therefore avoided sight of the man? Now she sealed in earnest that withdrawal from Bowles and from nearly everybody else. At the same time her creative life surged to its full. What she had to do, as to Bowles, was to get so she "could hear his name—/ Without—Tremendous gain—/That Stop-sensation—on my soul—/And Thunder—in the Room."

She sent him poems, books, letters. "Please to need me." Perhaps it was one day in 1865 when again Bowles had been in the Dickinson house and Emily, not seeing him, wrote at once "I went to the room as soon as you left, to confirm your presence . . .

" 'I have no life but this . . .
The love of you.' "

She wrote him: "The last day that I saw you was the newest and oldest of my life." Also: "You have the most triumphant face out of Paradise, probably because you are there constantly, instead of ultimately." One letter, in 1873, refers to her having seen him again.

In January, 1878, Bowles died in his fifty-second year. Emily was then forty-seven. On the day of Bowles's funeral, which Austin and Lavinia Dickinson attended, Emily wrote Higginson: "The last song that I heard—that was, since the birds—was 'He leadeth me, he leadeth me; yea, though I walk'—then the voices stooped, the arch was so low." A year later she wrote Higginson that her father's death "and the passing of Mr. Bowles, and mother's hopeless illness, overwhelmed my moments."

Sometimes Emily wrote to Mary Bowles. "As he was himself Eden, he is with Eden." (Richard Chase has noted that Emily habitually refers to home as "Eden.") She hopes his children resemble Bowles, "that his beautiful face may be abroad." In 1881, in her last known letter to Mrs. Bowles, she acknowledges a photograph of one of the children: "the beautiful face . . . and the look of Arabia in the eyes is like Mr. Samuel." In the 1880's she sometimes wrote to the son Samuel and once to Charles—her "Robert"—now engaged to be married. In 1882 Emily wrote a friend, "I dreamed Saturday night of precious Mr. Bowles. One glance of his would light the world." Was this not the face, "the most triumphant face out of Paradise," that for Emily at Resurrection "would put out Jesus' "?

A few things remain to be said; first of all to raise the delicate question of the ambiguity of Emily's relationship with Mrs. Samuel Bowles. The answer is twofold: we have assumed all along that the man with whom Emily fell in love was married, and we interpret from the record that Emily's solution was to avoid seeing him—perhaps her self-imposed retreat was an extension of a particularized exile.

We also know, from Mrs. Bingham's *Emily Dickinson: A Revelation,* that there were contemporary judgments of Emily which rated her shabbily. Mabel Loomis Todd said that Austin Dickinson's wife, Susan, warned her neither Emily nor her sister Lavinia had "any idea of morality. . . . 'I went in there one day, and in the drawing room I found Emily reclining in the arms of a man. What do you say to that?' " This was in 1881, about the time of Emily's impassioned letters to Judge Lord, who used to visit her. And fifty years later the Judge's ancient niece yammered at Mrs. Bingham that Emily was a "little hussy—didn't I know her? I should say I did. Loose morals. She was crazy about men. Even tried to get Judge Lord. Insane, too."

These cattish remarks, however excessive, have the value of reminding us that though we think of Emily Dickinson as a great poet, she was also a woman. In her lifetime, as John Erskine discovered, she was regarded "without enthusiasm by the neighbors she ignored or scorned." She was capable, like most women, of crushes. She was capable, like many women, of falling in love more than once.

There is the question, if my theory about Samuel Bowles is correct, why has it gone unstated all these years? The answer is that most writers on Emily Dickinson have leaped at a theory of identification and have been so bent on fitting the facts to it that they have had to miscast Samuel Bowles. And yet the most capable of the theorists, Genevieve Taggard, with her George Gould error, went so far as to think Emily was "almost" in love with Bowles.

Probably a part of the answer is that to allege Emily's love for a married man nearby, a man whose wife she knew and whose children she knew all about, a man who frequented the Dickinson house, is to uncover a more compromising, a more embarrassing triangle than that posited by the mistily-mythical, far-removed Wadsworth. Another way of putting it: a more real triangle. The Wadsworth theory makes noble reading devoid of unpleasantness. There is a very unpleasant streak, as in real life, in the Bowles theory. The uncommitted Mrs. Bingham obviously regards Bowles as a possibility, obviously is dubious about the Rev. Charles Wadsworth.

The case for Wadsworth, as I have shown, rests on conjecture. It relies heavily on a group of letters Emily wrote to his friends after Wadsworth's death, letters inquiring affectionately for details of his life and family. She seems rather less than well informed about him. She admired him greatly. She referred to him as "my dearest earthly friend." I think we can underline the word *friend*. At this very time she was deeply in love with Judge Lord. His wife had died in 1877, the year before Samuel Bowles. Emily's passion for the Judge apparently dates circa 1880 until his death in 1884. Wadsworth died in 1882, Emily Dickinson in 1886.

Finally, despite all the precedents, one must make some apology for this sort of prying. I quote Henry James: "Nothing more generally or more recurrently solicits us, in the light of literature, I think, than the interest of our learning how the poet, the true poet, and above all the particular one with whom for the moment we may be concerned, has come into his estate, asserted and preserved his identity, worked out his question of sticking to that and to nothing else; and has so been able to reach us and touch us *as* a poet, in spite of the accidents and dangers that must have beset this course." Most of the great love poetry in English has been written by men and most of it out of love unpossessed or lost. Emily Dickinson uniquely domesticated her contribution: the words "husband" and "wife" and "marriage" are for her magic words, passionate and beautiful words. The poems remain of first importance. But to specify the central experience from which the greatest of them flowered—"I cannot live with You / It would be Life—"—is to understand more clearly how she came into her estate and by what way she reached to touch us.

Winfield Townley Scott is a one-time literary editor (of the Providence Journal*), a part-time New Englander (he now lives in Santa Fe), and a full-time poet (eight volumes). This study of Emily Dickinson will appear in* Exiles and Fabrications, *a book of essays mainly about New England authors and places, to be published in August by Doubleday.*

Samuel Bowles

PHOTOGRAPH CREDITS:

100: © HARPER & BROTHERS

102: PRESBYTERIAN HISTORICAL ASSOC., PHILADELPHIA

103, 105: CULVER PICTURES, INC.

PHOTOGRAPHS JULIA KNOWLTON

THE SAND CASTLE

As backs go, the one in the photograph at left is most expressive. The satisfied stance, the hands on the hips, are those of the architect well pleased with his handiwork; but there is more to it than that. Observe the knowing set of the head as it gauges the approaching combers: one more, or certainly two or three, and the green tongues of bubbling surf will lick around the moat of this sandy Mont-Saint-Michel, obliterate the terraces, undermine the walls; until, a few waves later, the battlements topple and the sea reclaims the builder's handiwork. Construction, so full of excitement and things to imagine; destruction, so devastating, so awe-inspiring—this is the stuff for an afternoon on the beach, especially if you are nine, serious-minded, and not given to wasting time as adults do on such foolishness as surf fishing (you hardly ever catch anything), sun bathing (how can they lie still so long?), drinking (it tastes awful), or romance (which is mush). There were adults around all afternoon doing silly things like that. A lot of them hung about staring, as though they'd never seen a castle before—you notice more about them than they think—but the grownups all rushed for their cars when it rained, and suddenly the beach was empty. Flabby lot, adults.

Such is the argument of *The Sand Castle,* a perceptive and unusual new motion picture written, produced, and directed by Jerome Hill, grandson of the great railroad builder James J. Hill, an artist, writer, and film maker who won an Academy Award for his movie *Albert Schweitzer*. The musical score is by Alec Wilder, who appears on screen as a fisherman. The story is deceptively simple, and the actual events are shown in black and white; but when the boy steals a nap beside his castle, his dreams come out in color: a real castle, himself the knight, and the people he has been quietly observing, its strange inhabitants. All this was done by Hill personally, in animation with paper figurines modeled on the nineteenth-century cardboard cutout theaters known, after the price of the cutouts, as "penny plain, tuppence colored." Not the smallest triumph of the film, however, is the sand castle itself, a subject to which (as his comments on the next pages show) Hill has given much deep thought. OLIVER JENSEN

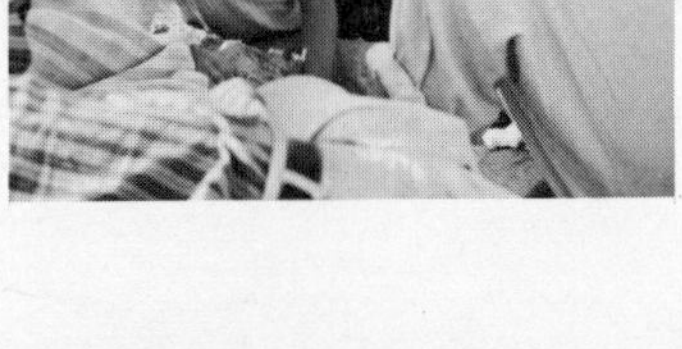

Film-maker Hill and his young star, Barry Caldwell, take a break on location at Laguna Beach, California. Barry is nine.

How to Build a Sand Castle

Like snow sculpture, sand-castle building is one of those ephemeral arts that, from the beginning of time, has been the nearly undisputed domain of children. Asked when I made my first castle, I have to admit that I can't remember. What is notable, I suppose, is that I never outgrew building them. The instructions which I shall now give, by this token, were probably once known to many of my readers and have been subsequently forgotten.

The length of time it takes to build a castle is roughly ten hours—the period between tides. One cannot begin to build until the water retreats. The grand finale is the washing away of the castle by the sea. It is against the unwritten rules to sidestep the ultimate destruction by building out of reach of the tide. There are good reasons for this. In the first place, sand of the required dampness would either lie too deep under the surface or would be too long a haul. Furthermore, the final undermining and washing away of the whole structure is an essential step and can even be considered the heart of the experience. Not that a well-built castle protected from the waves by a stout rampart won't last in all its clear-cut beauty for days. The very act of pressing and cutting the sand transforms the tiny grains into an almost cementlike material resembling stale cake. No, the destructive element, alas, is neither sun nor wind nor water—none of the elements, in short, but birds and men. Sea gulls delight in perching on the ramparts, and with their awkward webbed feet, level the tiny houses. Dogs, for some unknown reason, have a certain respect for sand castles—but people, no! An unattended castle, discovered by a band of immature human beings, is an invitation to vandalism. The sensible builder, then, will stay with his creation from its inception to its final annihilation.

The best sand is found just below the crest of the beach, on the sea side, and is of exactly the right consistency fifteen minutes or so after the last retreating wave has left it.

Two or three people are not too many to help form the basic pile. Shovels, real shovels, are almost a necessity. A rough outline (preferably asymmetrical, about ten or twelve feet in diameter) having been traced, a ditch is dug outside this. All the material that comes out of this ditch should be deposited in the circumscribed area. It cannot be sufficiently stressed that each layer of this loose, damp stuff must be patted down firmly either with the open hand and forearm or with a flat paddle or stick. Treading it as if it were a grape harvest is a poor shortcut. This procedure loosens the sand and makes holes in it. The finished basic pile should be about three feet high, and an hour or two can easily be consumed in completing this stage.

It is sometimes hard on the faithful helpers who have been digging and patting to step aside and do nothing while the master builder takes over and carves the castle; consequently the highest part of the mound should be completed first, and then the sculptor can begin on it while the other workers finish the subsidiary knolls and outer slopes. The castle must be shaped from the top down and from the center out, so that the builder doesn't get in his own way. A variety of tools is desirable, the most useful being a small beach pail, to mold the towers, and a good strong mason's trowel with one straight edge, to cut away

These are scenes
from the movie:
build a little castle
and pretty soon
you have a big crowd

Help from sister

Stares from the oddest people

Power of concentration

Mother Superior flyed-out in the moat

Master builders need rest

the walls. Various cooking utensils have special uses—a narrow spatula to remove the sand between buttresses, a pancake turner for roofs and leveling. A square-ended putty knife will shape a good flight of stairs. Pieces of driftwood of varying lengths can be used for terracing.

I have never copied an already existing castle, but with the aid of a photograph, it could undoubtedly be done. It's much more fun to improvise. Whether one intends it or not, the very material used leads one inevitably to a style best exemplified by the great stone and mortar masterpieces of the Middle Ages, found all over Europe and the Near East—Mont-Saint-Michel, Carcassonne, the Italian hill towns, are good models. A broken arch will stand better than a round one; wall openings cannot be indefinitely enlarged. A high escarpment will collapse if it is not supported by proper buttressing. From an engineering standpoint, the secrets of the Romanesque and Gothic styles are revealed very clearly to the sand architect.

To begin, then, at the top of the highest mound: level and pat an area approximately one foot square.

Fill a bucket with loose, damp sand. To solidify it from the bottom up, tap the full bucket against the ground several times. If the level of sand in the bucket drops, fill in with new loose sand and continue tapping.

Turn it upside down on the truncated summit of the pile.

Before removing the bucket, pat out any cracks that have been caused by the upside-down-cake operation.

When the pail is slipped vertically up and off, the carving can begin. At this initial point one can afford to be very bold. Lofty tapering spires are not out of the question, but the square English cathedral-type belfry is, of course, safer. When the large central structures are finished, there is a special charm in surrounding them with smaller houses to give them scale and then adding outer walls with ramps and towers. The lowest slopes can be finished off with terracing on which seaweed fragments, planted in rows, will suggest orchards.

In anticipation of the final moment of destruction, it's a good idea to hollow out a deep channel which will introduce the first wave that arrives directly to the back of the castle and even around it. This river, or moat, can be crossed by bridges, and this is where engineering problems are most directly met. Reinforcement for long spans can be made with embedded sticks or seaweed, but the more simple, well-designed, single-arched bridge with a slightly crowned top is better.

When we were kids, we turned the final phase, the demolition, into a game. Each builder indicated the tower or house that he thought would last the longest. As his particular construction collapsed, he dropped a coin into a hat. The last man won the kitty.

The crowds, so familiar in our cities, who gather to watch the activities of a building site—and even more, those who wouldn't miss a fire—are the same who stand transfixed in front of the sand-castle a-building. For the creator, the rather indefinable pleasure derived is not unconnected with the fact that such a permanent-looking structure on so ambitious a scale can be made in so short a time, and disappears so dramatically and so completely.

JEROME HILL

What is that boy doing?

Here's a tin knight for your castle!

Sidewalk superintendents

Recorded on canvas

When the tide returns

The end has a noble quality

LOU MYERS'S PHILOSOPHICAL PRIMER

Not long ago Lou Myers, an American cartoonist who had long worked in Paris, returned home and for his own edification took a course in philosophy. Finding many propositions and principles as given in standard works wordy and confusing, he reduced them to brief illustrations of his own, with the results on these pages.

STOICISM
the virtuous man is free from passion, unmoved by joy or pain

SKEPTICISM
knowledge is unattainable, and if attained is unrecognizable

UTILITARIANISM
the right act will produce the happiest results

OPTIMISM
the world is good and man's destiny bright

IDEALISM

the pursuit of perfection whether or not attainable

EMPIRICISM

the sole source of knowledge is experience

PESSIMISM

the world is bad and man's destiny dark

LouMyers

BOOKS

Poor Winnie in Pooh-Latin

In December, 1960, the adventurous firm of Dutton published a little book which anyone could have told them would never sell more than a few dozen copies. It was a Latin translation of a British children's book: *Winnie-the-Pooh*, by A. A. Milne. The original was more than thirty years old, although still popular. Its author was dead; the little boy he wrote about had grown up long ago and was dead too; many modern children cared little for stories about a child who carried about a Teddy bear and talked with it. Certainly none of them could read a hundred and twenty pages of Latin like this: "*Suspiria duxerunt et consurrexerunt; deinde spinis nonnullis vepris e natibus evulsis ad mutua dicta reddenda consederunt.*" Any boy or girl who was knowledgeable enough to get through that, in the United States at least, would be more interested in sex, sports, and spaceships than in toy kangaroos and stuffed donkeys; and only a wildly eccentric parent would buy the Latin version of the book, *Winnie ille Pu*, in order to read it to his children, translating as he went along, when the original English, with all the same illustrations, was available at the same price or less. The book had, it seemed, no chance of succeeding.

To make things worse, no one had ever heard of the translator. Perhaps an eminent wit (say, Peter Ustinov, who can imitate all languages) or a famous author (such as T. S. Eliot, who has written some pleasant poems about pet animals) might have turned out a Latin version of a children's book and made it sell by the prestige of his name. But *Winnie ille Pu* was translated by a European physician who, when his book was issued here, was living in a remote part of Brazil; so that no one could say the book had been helped by the glamour of a name. (On the other hand, Dutton was once before very lucky with a book by an unknown European physician named Axel Munthe.)

Yet by the spring of 1961 the translation had sold more than sixty thousand copies and had made its way onto several best-seller lists. It looked odd to see, alongside the tormented Jews of *The Last of the Just* and the corrupt union leaders of *Midcentury*, the plump bear and the battered piglet, wearing the heavy uniforms of Roman legionaries; but there they were. An eminent classical scholar read selections from *Winnie ille Pu*, in Latin, to the audience of a highly cultivated radio station. News magazines called up university Latin departments to ask for an interpretation of the phenomenon: Did it mean that Latin was "coming back"? No one could really explain it; but the enterprising Dutton company continued to manufacture and sell the little book; for, as Martial said of an earlier best seller,

Sunt quidam qui me dicant non esse poetam
sed qui me vendit bibliopola putat.

However, the thing was not unique. It had been done before, although not in America and seldom if ever on such a scale. In Italy there was a successful Latin version of a favorite children's book: *Pinoculus*. Long ago I seem to have seen a Latin version of the German tales about those ancestors of the Katzenjammer kids, Max und Moritz. In England the practice of writing and publishing translations of unusual poems and stories, into both Latin and Greek, has had a firm hold for at least a century and shows no sign of weakening. The English have always enjoyed puzzle making and puzzle solving. (They like crosswords far more than we do, and they like them to be really ingenious: e.g., "Irish author around forty" = AXLE; or, "Arkwright was his father" = SHEM. These examples come from Charles P. Curtis's delightful *Commonplace Book*.) Also, any Englishman who goes to a "good" school and takes classics is taught, at what we should think a very early age, to write Greek and

Latin prose and verse. If he aspires to win any university distinctions in classical studies, he must be prepared to face examination papers which require him, without a dictionary at his side, without any books whatever, (a) to turn part of Satan's first speech in *Paradise Lost* into Latin hexameters, (b) to produce a Greek-verse equivalent of the fourth section of Eliot's *The Waste Land,* (c) to put Housman's poem "Loveliest of Trees" into either Latin or Greek lyrics, and (d) if he has still time and energy within the three-hour limit, to put some of Dryden's *Absalom and Achitophel* into the rhythms and vocabulary of Latin satire.

After one acquires some skill at this kind of thing, it is hard to stop doing it. If one teaches Greek and Latin, one goes on naturally to tackle more and more tantalizing problems in translation for the pleasure of solving them. One of the finest pieces of poetic translation I have ever had the privilege of reading is Sir Maurice Bowra's conversion of Coleridge's *Kubla Khan* into a Greek ode in the manner of Pindar. Mgr. Ronald Knox (Eton and Balliol), who was one of the finest "composers" of his generation, published some translations into Greek and Latin verse of English pieces which most expert scholars would have pronounced untranslatable.

Every month, in the British classical teachers' magazine *Greece and Rome,* there appear several new Greek and Latin translations of unusually difficult English (or even French and German) poems. A complete translation into Latin elegiac couplets of Lewis Carroll's *Hunting of the Snark* (of which an excerpt appears on the following page) was published in the 1930's; and very soon after *Alice in Wonderland* first appeared, a Cambridge classicist produced a version of "Jabberwocky" which still stands up beautifully. In our own day Mgr. Knox improved on this feat by turning the poem into Greek iambics, as though it were a fragment of a newly discovered tragedy; an excerpt from this translation also appears overleaf.

A short ballad in regular four-line stanzas, "Jabberwocky" is formally not difficult to turn into Latin couplets. Its chief problem is that it is full of new "portmanteau" words, which are made up of two or more real words squeezed into one, as clothes are squeezed together in a portmanteau. For instance, the "toves," if you remember, are "slithy," which means both lithe and slimy. In Latin "lithe" is *gracilis,* and "slimy" is *lubricus*: so the toves are *"lubriciles,"* which fits beautifully into dactylic verse. The moment of victory, "through and through the vorpal blade went snicker-snack," produces a lovely pentameter: *"persnicuit gladio persnacuitque puer."*

It was this taste for problem solving, and for using Latin not only as a "tool" for reading but as a toy for playing with, that created the new translation of *Winnie-the-Pooh.* That was why Dr. Lenard wrote it, and that is why people buy it—although whether they ever read it, I cannot tell. If they do, they have warm hearts and soft heads.

The real trouble is that Dr. Lenard's translation is not good. It has little of the charm of the original. It has too much dubious or bad Latin in it. It is seldom witty. It fails to solve most of the really interesting problems of interpretation.

To begin with, the title *Winnie ille Pu* is a miserable rendering of "Winnie-the-Pooh." Winnie is a girl's name, short for Winifred; the bear was soft and winning. Pooh used to be the name of a pet swan owned by Christopher Robin —probably a floating toy for the bath— and then passed to his Teddy bear; apparently it is child's talk for "pet," "specially loved toy," and might be allied with "puss." (I have heard at least one pet kitten called Pussy Poo.) Therefore anyone who starts translating such a book should make an imaginative effort to produce a real Latin version of its hero's name. "Honey" was good Latin baby talk for a beloved person, the little bear loved honey, so why not call him *Melculus*? It is a word guaranteed by the authority of the Emperor Augustus himself. As for Pooh, Dr. Lenard was wise enough to avoid *Pus,* but he would have done better to use a playful Latin word for "tiny" such as *pusillus* or *pupus* or *pupulus.*

Of course *ille* does not mean "the." It means "that." Caesar the Dictator is not *Caesar ille Dictator,* but simply *Caesar Dictator.* Peter Pan is *Petrus Pan,* not *Petrus ille Pan;* Laurence the star is not *Laurentius ille Stella,* but simply *Laurentius Stella.* Even if you are so misguided as to use *ille* for part of your hero's name, you remember that it takes various shapes in different relationships, accusative, genitive, and so forth; and you do not dream of writing *"audivi Winnie ille Pum,"* as Dr. Lenard does; you decline the word properly and write *"illum."*

Perhaps Dr. Lenard does not understand the subtleties of English any better than he seems to know the little delicacies of Latin. He calls the donkey *Ior,* which looks like a sound classical name: there was a hero called Ion and an unhappy lady called Io; still, in Latin the name sounds rather Greek and quite meaningless. Christopher Robin's donkey was called Eeyore, which, with a heavily English pronunciation, comes out "Hee-haw," the donkey's characteristic cry. A good translator would have tried to carry this effect across into the other language. For instance, one nice word for the donkey's bray was *oncare,* so why not call Eeyore *Onca*? It is more onomatopoeic and more grotesquely comic than *Ior.*

The actual translation is very far away from the original. A. A. Milne wrote light, bright, conversational English; much of it was talk, in childish language or simple slang, between toy animals; and much of it was clearly the language of an affectionate father telling a story to his little boy. Dr. Lenard writes heavy, complicated Latin, full of words which the average Roman adult —to say nothing of small children— never heard or used in his entire life, plastered with pompous "constructions" half-remembered from manuals of Latin grammar, and full of awkward mistakes. (Some of them may be due to his own careless proofreading, some to the printers, some, possibly, to the publishers' zeal. Messrs. Dutton have added some new boners, both on the jacket of the book and in their publicity handouts, one of which actually manages to introduce a blunder into the first four words of Caesar's *Gallic War*.)

The translation could have been understood by a Roman—apart from some words which are to be found in no reputable Latin dictionary, like *sclopetum* for "gun"—but he would have thought that the writer was some kind of extraordinary foreigner who combined astonishing ignorance with astounding pedantry, and he would have got very little impression of the genuine charm of Pooh and his friends, which depends on their simplicity. You have probably seen those excerpts from English-language summaries of Japanese plays and motion pictures which *The New Yorker* sometimes prints under the caption "The Mysterious East." If you have, you will understand what Dr. Lenard's *Winnie ille Pu* would look like to a Roman. A comical little sentence like the donkey's protest, "All this washing," becomes something appropriate to a fourth-century Christian bishop commenting on the spiritual effects of baptism, *"Ecce, quod ex ablutionibus evenire solet."* (No little Roman boy, or his toy animals, ever dreamed of using the word *ablutio*.) Poor old Pooh's pathetically simple plea, *"What about meals?"* turns out as *"Et quid, quod ad refectiones attinet?"* To a Roman this would be a suitable question to address to an architect in an official meeting, and would sound something like "And, with reference to restorations . . . ?"

In Chapter II we find the Pooh bear trying to touch, in Latin, his ***hallux***. This is really far-fetched. The word does not occur once, not once, in all the thousands of pages of Latin literature. It is known only from a few compilers of very special dictionaries, and even they were not quite sure what it meant.

Now That Classical Languages Are "In" Again—

In order to provide readers of his above critique of *Winnie ille Pu* with some examples of good recent renderings of English verse into ancient tongues, Gilbert Highet here offers a brief anthology of some he likes best, giving the classicized version below the originals. In the far right-hand column, opposite, another contemporary exercise in Latin is added in the form of a quatrain composed to assist those desirous of memorizing the precise numerical value of the formula π that expresses the ratio of the circumference of a circle to its diameter. Although the rough value of π was first ascertained in classical times, its further decimals were not worked out until our own; to have these now glossed in literary Latin may be still another indication that the humanities and the sciences are coming together again.

The accursèd power which stands on Privilege
(And goes with Women, and Champagne and Bridge)
Broke—and Democracy resumed her reign:
(Which goes with Bridge, and Women and Champagne).

Hilaire Belloc

Κότταβον οἳ πόρνας τε μέθην τ' ἐφίλησαν, ἀπεχθεῖς
πᾶσιν, ἐρειδόμενοι δεσποσύνοις γέρασιν,
ἐξέπεσον· δήμου δὲ φίλοι πόλιν αὖθις ἔχουσιν,
οἷσι φίλαι πόρναι, κότταβος ἠδὲ μέθη.

C. M. Bowra, *Some Oxford Compositions*
(Clarendon; Oxford, 1949)

THE HUNTING OF THE SNARK

FIT THE FIRST: THE LANDING

"Just the place for a Snark!" The Bellman cried,
As he landed his crew with care;
Supporting each man on the top of the tide
By a finger entwined in his hair.

"Just the place for a Snark! I have said it twice:
That alone should encourage the crew.
Just the place for a Snark! I have said it thrice:
What I tell you three times is true."

Lewis Carroll

SNARCIS VENATIO

CAPVT PRIMVM: EX NAVE EGRESSUS

"Hic locus est!" dicit "Snarci haec aptissima sedes!"
Dum Stentor comites extrahit ipse mari,
Sollicitus nantes summo quos sustinet aestu,
Implicitas digito corripiente comas.

"Hic Snarcis locus est, sic vox fremit ecce secunda,
Sola meos debet quae stimulare viros.
Hic Snarcis locus est; sic vox mea tertia clamat,
Voce ter emissa non dubitanda loquor.

H. D. Watson, ***The Hunting of the Snark***
translated into Latin Elegiacs (Blackwell; Oxford, 1936)

One thought it meant a sixth finger on an abnormal hand; another thought it was a toe; and another said authoritatively that it was a thumb encroaching on the first finger (whatever that means). Certainly it is not the correct and easy Latin for a little bear's toe, and only a pedant with no feeling for language would have dreamed of using a word so recondite in a simple, pleasant storybook.

Even nice, simple, analphabetic Christopher Robin cannot say "Then you had better have the blue balloon" to his Pooh bear in Dr. Lenard's Latin without beginning *"Quod cum ita sit,"* as though he were an elderly Roman magistrate proposing a motion, and going on into a heavy gerundive with a *"folliculus est praeferendus,"* as though he were Cato talking about Carthage. Oliver Goldsmith said of Dr. Johnson that, if he were to make little fishes talk, they would talk like whales. Dr. Lenard has made a little boy and his pet animals speak, not real Latin, not the Latin in which children played games and parents told them stories, but bishop-Latin, pedant-Latin, whale-Latin, dinosaur-Latin. It might have been funny to do the Swiss Family Robinson (who often speak rather pompously) in this stodgy and sesquipedalian Latin; but not Pooh and his pleasant little friends.

Well, these are trifling criticisms, but it is a trifling book. It was no doubt created as a personal hobby, by a lonely man with an eccentric taste. If it had been well done, it would have been a harmless pastime. As it is, anyone who has a feel for language and reads *Winnie ille Pu* must feel like an admirer of sailing ships who, when shown a ship in a bottle, sees that it lacks a rudder, is wearing an anachronistic radio antenna, has some Band-Aid patches on its hull, and that it has its mainsail adrift. When a thing is intended to be useless, it ought at least to be elegant.

GILBERTUS CRITICUS
(Gilbert Highet)

JABBERWOCKY

'Twas brillig, and the slithy toves
  Did gyre and gimble in the wabe;
All mimsy were the borogroves,
  And the mome raths outgrabe.

"Beware the Jabberwock, my son!
  The jaws that bite, the claws that catch!
Beware the Jubjub bird, and shun
  The frumious Bandersnatch!"

Lewis Carroll

ΙΑΜΒΡΩΞ ΙΑΜΒΙΚΩΣ

Καυσπροῦντος ἤδη, γλοῖσχρα διὰ περισκιᾶς
στρυβλοῦντα καὶ στρομφοῦντ᾿ ἂν εὑρίσκοις τόφα,
δεινὴ δ᾿ ἐπέσχε σωθρία βορυγρόφας,
ῥάθαισι δ᾿ ἀντιποικὸν ὕμνησαν ῥάθαι
ἔκγριμμα· τὸν δὲ πρέσβυν ἐξαυδᾶν κλύω·
'παῖ, παῖ, φύγοις ἂν ἐμπέδως Ἰάμβροχα,
εἴτ᾿ ὄνυχι μάρπτων εἴτε δὴ δάκνων τύχοι
γνάθοισιν, ἀπρόσοιστον· ὧς δ᾿ αὔτως φυγεῖν
ὄρνιθα δεινὸν Γυπογῦπ᾿· οὐδ᾿ ἂν φθάνοις
ἔλθων δαφλοισβῷ πρὸς λόγους Βανδράρπαγι."

Ronald Knox, *In Three Tongues*
(Chapman and Hall; London, 1959)

A MNEMONIC FOR THE VALUE OF π

The value of π, carried to thirty decimal places, is 3.14159-265358979323846264338 3279. In order to assist a schoolmate and friend of his (who preferred mathematics to classical languages) to memorize the formula, Father Ronald Knox, the Roman Catholic theologian, classicist, and wit at Oxford, devised for his friend Bailey the following Latin poem. Each word, by the number of letters it contains, denotes a figure, and the succession of these figures coincides with the succession of decimals of π. The integer "3" is purposely omitted; those ignorant of this can remember it by memorizing the number of initials in the author's name (RRK).

To Mr. H. Bailey

1 4 1 5 9 2 6 5
I nunc, O Baili, Parnassum et desere rupem;

3 5 8 9 7
Dic sacra Pieridum deteriora quadris!

9 3 2 3 8 4 6 2 6
Subsidium hoc ad vos, quamquam leve, fertur ab hymnis

4 3 3 8 3 2 7 9
Quos dat vox Sophocli (non in utroque probrumst?)

"Will you dare any longer, Bailey, to turn your back on Parnassus hill, telling us that the sacred rites of the Muses are less important than constructing squares? Here is aid brought to you, though it be but slight, by poetry, and poetry couched in the language of Sophocles—there is a double thrust at your vanity!"

Ronald Knox, *In Three Tongues*
(Chapman and Hall; London, 1959)

Arise, Ye Playgoers of the World

Western drama was created to celebrate legends and perpetuate mysteries, and plays were housed in the porches of cathedrals before they had homes of their own. I hope I will not spoil anyone's fun, therefore, if I point out that, more than other literary forms, the theater has reached its peaks in an atmosphere of moral vehemence. Novelists and poets have often written out of a sense of outrage and a passion for improvement, but few of them have dared to wag a finger with the open assurance of Ibsen, Strindberg, Shaw, or Bertolt Brecht. Molière cloaked homily in wit; Shakespeare ticked off the major vices with the zeal of a catechist. In our day Tennessee Williams has lectured almost exclusively on moral dyspepsia, illustrating his talks with charts as lurid as any displayed by the Anti-Saloon League. A playwright's great advantage over other writers is that he speaks to congregations. Only the preacher enenjoys the same power, and beneath the different trappings of place and circumstance the message is the same: "Go, and sin no more." Implicit in a sermon is the belief that people can be awakened to take action against their moral decay.

The shock we have experienced recently in the theater comes, I think, in considerable part from the fact that several of the most forceful writers have foregone their hortatory role and become dispassionate chroniclers of humanity's swift and irreversible decline. In such plays as *The Chairs, The Balcony,* and *Endgame* the playwrights Ionesco, Genet, and Beckett, with varying degrees of directness and in contexts of humor, disgust, or pity related to their own personalities, have been telling their audiences that social decay has passed considerably beyond the point where exhortation would be relevant. A preacher could devise no more devastating act than to take a bowl of water with him into the pulpit and there wash his hands of the congregation. It might also be the most therapeutic act he could devise (and some such motive may lie beneath the exploits of the above-mentioned writers), but it would be abnormal, desperate, and vitiated by repetition.

Therefore it had seemed to me that these writers—I would add John Osborne because his work, though styled in what looks like the theater of protest, is in fact a counsel of revulsion—were engaged in so violent a dislocation of the theater's natural course that a return to the tradition of moral suasion was predictable. Some of the most interesting work of the past not very interesting season suggests that this is happening.

What started me thinking along these lines were two one-act plays by Edward Albee: *The Death of Bessie Smith* and *The American Dream.* For Albee, whose moral fervor is as urgent as a war cry, writes in the vernacular of the Theater of the Absurd, another name for the disengagement of Ionesco-Genet-Beckett. The heroine of *Bessie Smith* is less a woman than a hieratic monster, akin to the three-nosed bride of Ionesco's *Jack.* The people of *The American Dream,* like Beckett's stumblers and gropers, are grotesquely deprived of their faculties, live in a setting of dreamlike anonymity, and agitate the audience into almost constant laughter by the irrelevance, incongruity, and ironic juxtapositions of their conversation. As with Beckett, our horror at the statement of an Albee play comes as an aftertaste; but, unlike Beckett, it comes as an admonition.

Bessie Smith, one of the great Negro blues singers, died in 1937 after an automobile accident near Memphis, Tennessee. She died in the street because the first white hospital to which she was taken would not admit her, and she did not survive to reach the second. It would be convenient, especially in the North, to suppose that Albee's play is about race prejudice, but the theme is not that easy (in the sense that most of us now have available an automatic and almost guiltless sense of indignation in the presence of discrimination).

Bessie Smith never appears in the play that bears her name, nor is her death its subject. The subject is mutilation as a substitute for love. The hospital nurse who dominates the action, growing rankly and unfruitfully in a sterile community, can reach out to the two men in her orbit only to blight them. The interne is white, the orderly Negro, but she amputates their pride and promise with cold impartiality. Her savagery is hysterical, a kind of perverse rape, and the men accept it because if they did not feel her knife, they would feel nothing at all.

When Bessie's gentleman friend storms into the office, he does not affront the staff because he is black; he frightens them because he is in honest agony. And when the orderly and interne return from the car outside, their hands are more covered with blood than you would think possible—unless, desperately and hopelessly, they had been washing in the ebbing life of Bessie Smith. Kenneth Tynan has expressed some scorn for the play as opposing discrimination because of its degenerative effect upon the whites. I think he misunderstands. Albee is alarmed by a general failure of the channels of awareness. an inability of the public body to regenerate itself.

Albee had also treated the subject of violence beating vainly on the breast of insensibility in the earlier *Zoo Story,* which first brought him public notice when it was presented in a double bill last year with *Krapp's Last Tape* (Beckett). Now, in *The American Dream,* produced in tandem with *Bessie Smith,* he shifted his preoccupation into a world of more evident fantasy and symbol, couching the play in a chilling humor that suggests an evening of high spirits in the morgue.

The American Dream combines elements of science fiction (in that several of the characters seem to have had their brains replaced by servomechanisms) with elements of Grand Guignol (in that a baby, adopted some years earlier by the couple of the play, had been reproved for his infant indiscretions by the surgical loss of each offending limb and organ). Not surprisingly, that baby died, and the adoption agent has finally shown up to replace it—with its teenage identical twin. This young man is The American Dream: seeming on the outside as succulent as an apple, but as crippled psychically as his brother had been surgically.

Allegories do not fare well in paraphrase, and I shall not do further damage to this one by completing the summary. The play's wild humor is occasioned by the fact that whereas the automatized characters respond with ludicrous precision to one another's clichés, any odd remark fails to stimulate the receiving mechanisms (and there are many odd remarks because the instruments are not equipped with censors). The machine folk are also egged on a bit by an old party named Grandma, who is both senile and crafty, and who enjoys the flexibility, even in her dotage, of being human. I got a bad scare at the end of this play by hearing, from the row behind me, some comments about *The American Dream* so insensitive, so brutal, that they differed in no essential quality from what had been coming earlier from the stage. As Grandma says when, stepping out of character, she freezes the action just before the final curtain, "This is a comedy and we had better stop it right here."

Albee is young, and his "promise" has become a catchword of the contemporary theater. He knows how to engender stage excitement, he can borrow without imitating, and he is beset by ideas. In his zeal to get a message across, he seems to put himself too evidently on the stage; and for a man otherwise so much at home in the theater, he has a surprisingly hard time with his endings. He tends to lurch in the home stretch, like a boy who has learned everything about riding a bike except how to get off.

In Arnold Wesker's *Roots,* the urge to preach becomes so insistent that the main character, Beatie Bryant, periodically hops up onto a table or chair, the better to harangue her associates and, of course, the audience. The trilogy, *Chicken Soup With Barley, Roots,* and *I'm Talking About Jerusalem,* has pushed Wesker in three years to the front rank of England's youngest theater generation. The pivotal figure of the three plays is Ronnie Kahn, a restaurant worker with a large collection of LP's and a deep contempt for the passivity of the masses. He thus immediately fits the Angry Young Man category invented by Osborne, Wain, Braine, *et al.* But Ronnie is also related to the placard-waving, *agitprop* heroes of the American thirties, when Clifford Odets was urging us to awake and picket. One reason why Wesker is an exciting playwright is that he has had the nerve to make Ronnie a man who is both fed up and a crusader. In *Jerusalem,* Ronnie's brother-in-law, a utopian socialist, gets caught in a petty theft. We have suffered recently from the conventionalized views of the young Jeremiahs; Wesker's people jump out of pigeonholes in an irritating way that is strikingly lifelike.

The trilogy spans the history of a lower middle class London Jewish family from 1936 to the present, and swings in political conviction from a communism espoused in the spirit of middle-European socialism to a restoration of the principles of William Morris, including garden crops and a distaste for machinery. Wesker himself, when he is not writing plays, exhorts the British trade unions to recognize that a regard for the economic welfare of their members is not enough. He declares that the great mass of the people is entirely outside the culture of its age (that, indeed, is why it is a mass), and he implores the unions to open theaters, support orchestras, underwrite publishing houses, sponsor exhibitions. Slogans and programs, he holds, are useless because they only enforce the monolithic conformity of the public. Individual awakening, a jump of the spark from man to man, is the only answer.

Roots is the most explicit statement of Wesker's position; the other plays deal more with dreams that failed. Ronnie does not appear in this middle play; he is represented instead by his girl, Beatie, who is visiting her farm-worker family and who, in anticipation of Ronnie's arrival, is stridently sounding the call to truth and beauty. Every third speech by Beatie is a quotation from Ronnie, often delivered from a perch. It is evident that she doesn't understand a fraction of what she is saying and just as evident that Ronnie, himself a spruced-up social illiterate, has been feeding her secondhand generalizations. Wesker is an unusual missionary in that he clearly expects no quick road to salvation. But the point of the play is that after Ronnie has welshed on his engagement, after the family has said its "I told you's" and has quite humanly scored off the arrogant city sister, Beatie is still talking—and suddenly talking in her own voice.

The play is vivid and poignant. The country people are far from clods, and though the author has fetched Beatie a terrible blow, he has measured it to her powers of recuperation. From about the time of Sartre's *No Exit,* playwrights have been closing all doors on their characters. Wesker, for whom the stage is again a pulpit, not a killing ground, leaves a way out.

The whole trilogy should be brought here. *Roots* by itself distorts Wesker's ideas by making them seem more naïve than they are. Without the other plays, moreover, Ronnie looks a villain, and that compromises the author's purpose. Ronnie is a latter-day everyman, faulty, confused, driven by the genius of self-dissatisfaction. He is a considerable creation; in his own Jewish way, the sort of man the Irish put on their stage.

Roots was not very well produced in New York; it is a difficult play to stage with American personnel. The kind of country worker Wesker describes does not exist here, and though our culture may be debased, it is not stagnant. Cut off from our roots, we racket all over the place; Wesker's people are withering, like marrows with their roots severed beneath them. The cast seemed to be visiting the play, not living in it; and the production, lacking a security of location and tone, fell off into staginess. Further, the young actress who played Beatie displayed the wrong kind of vitality. She suggested a sociology major on a rampage, and since much of what she mouthed was platitudinous, she sounded more stupid than ignorant. Wesker does not waste pity on stupidity; he is the champion of the uninformed.

But despite a fallible production, and although I have reservations about the Wesker gospel, *Roots* goes on ringing in my ears as few plays have recently. Causes make theater, but you needn't join up to enjoy their power. Shaw did well for the stage, but anyone who swore allegiance to his banner would have lost his mind before half the plays were staged.

The season in New York saw another play, *Call Me by My Rightful Name* by Michael Shurtleff, in which a character ascends—this time a stepladder—to admonish the benighted. The story is of two students, one white, one Negro, who think that their friendship has surmounted the hostilities and guilts of prejudice, but who discover, when the chips of sexual jealousy are down, that it is not so. I like the boldness with which Shurtleff lays out his story; I would have admired the play still more had I not felt that its insights were more routine than its manner.

All the plays here mentioned were produced off Broadway. A couple of years ago, the future of off-Broadway theater seemed more than dubious because it was not finding playwrights; everyone agreed that it could not live indefinitely on the established repertory. But new plays are now popping up like toadstools; the mortality, as with toadstools, is high, but the theater is a difficult and wasteful medium.

ROBERT HATCH

ADVERTISING

Would You Want Your Sister to Marry Rosser Reeves?

In his heart of hearts the advertising man is not terribly demanding. He asks little of life: a good income, a few acres in Westport, a corner office with several windows, and in the fullness of time, perhaps a carpet on the floor. Oh, and a little bit of love.

Since most of this is reasonably possible, it has come as something of a shock along Madison Avenue to realize that the little bit of love may be hard to come by. This has been callously revealed in a series of articles in *Advertising Age,* in which an account is given of a sincere kind of study made by an organization called Market Psychology Inc. In a spirit of honest inquiry, or perhaps of peevishness, Market Psychology Inc. was set the task of learning (1) what advertising men thought of themselves and (2) what their neighbors thought of them, by conducting interviews in the ad man's very lairs, such as Westport itself. When the results were in, *Advertising Age* gulped but published them.

One product was what *Advertising Age* calls "Profile of the 'Advertising Man,'" and it contains much to marvel over. For example, only 8 per cent of the ad men themselves thought of their fellow practitioners as "honest, straightforward." But that was a vote of confidence compared to what their neighbors thought: there the figure was a resounding 0 per cent. For the rest, ad men thought of themselves on the whole as energetic (71 per cent), bright young men (71 per cent), interested in ideas (96 per cent), trend-setters (74 per cent), original and creative (93 per cent), extroverted (76 per cent), and aggressive (64 per cent). Their neighbors, on the other hand, thought of ad men as interested in ideas (51 per cent), original and creative (67 per cent), extroverted (61 per cent), glib and superficial (59 per cent), neurotic (53 per cent), and heavy drinkers (53 per cent).

The interview included one question which presumably was intended to serve as summary for all the rest: "Whom would you prefer to have your sister marry?" The answer showed a distinct repugnance among the neighbors on behalf of their sisters where advertising men are concerned. A mere 4 per cent looked kindly upon the notion of having an ad man for a brother-in-law, whereas 67 per cent held out for a self-employed professional, and 18 per cent were willing to make do with a manufacturer. Among men who know the ad men best, it's self-employed professionals 17 to 1.

The worst of this is that just as things are at their darkest, a member of the advertising fraternity high up in the pecking order has come forth with a book. The author is Rosser Reeves, Chairman of the Board of Ted Bates & Company, and his book is called *Reality in Advertising*. Mr. Reeves, it should be said in his own defense, did not set out to write a book. He simply scribbled down a few ideas and rubbed them on the cat to see if she would lick them off. Much to his delight, he was immediately beset by associates who insisted that to withhold this magnum opus from the general public would be a major crime, like jaywalking.

The principal theme of the book is beyond reproof. It implies that anyone who has a dollar or two to spend in advertising, and who does not immediately turn it over to Mr. Reeves, is a thoroughgoing ass and will get what he deserves. Mr. Reeves develops this theme for 154 pages and from time to time gets pretty worked up about it. But this does not seem to be an unreasonable position for Mr. Reeves to maintain, for diffidence does not make a man Chairman of the Board.

Mr. Reeves's second major point is that harsh irritants, although they are no Unique Selling Proposition for cigarettes, are just the thing for advertising. ("Unique Selling Proposition" is Mr. Reeves's own phrase for "gimmick.") He is a voluble defender of the course of action that pushed George Washington Hill to the top of the heap: annoy people constantly enough and long enough, and they are likely to remember the name of your product. The worst of this is that it is probably true.

However neither of these is the salient feature of the book, although they begin to suggest it. What Mr. Reeves has managed to create is an image of advertising, and of the men who people it, that is warranted to make any right-thinking man lock his sister in the nearest closet. And Mr. Reeves is totally unaware of this, which makes it all the more engaging. He clearly considers the advertising man to be a composite of Albert Schweitzer, David Ricardo, and Sir Isaac Newton, but with only the best feature of each. He is not content with his opinion; he gives examples of advertising greatness. Let us quote him directly and print his own list of "the great advertising campaigns," presenting them, as he does, in capital letters:

" 'HALITOSIS' . . . 'LIFEBUOY AND B.O.' . . . 'L.S.M.F.T. AND THE CHANT OF THE TOBACCO AUCTIONEER' . . . 'IT'S TOASTED' . . . 'WHICH TWIN HAS THE TONI' . . . 'THOSE THREE STREAMS OF BUBBLES WHICH PROVE ANACIN BETTER THAN ASPIRIN OR BUFFERIN' . . . 'THOSE FLAVOR BUDS FOR MAXWELL HOUSE COFFEE' . . . 'WONDER BREAD HELPS BUILD STRONG BODIES 12 WAYS' . . . THAT OLD "FILM ON TEETH" CAMPAIGN OF CLAUDE HOPKINS . . . 'COLGATE DENTAL CREAM CLEANS YOUR BREATH WHILE IT CLEANS YOUR TEETH.' "

Now, having set down such a list, many a man would stop to apologize. But not Mr. Reeves. He continues: "The great campaigns, like the burning glass, fuse together all the components into a copy focus that generates not only light, but heat." I am not complaining about that sentence—I can't, because I haven't even a dim notion of what it means. It is the note of pride that appalls me. Mr. Reeves's hero is a man who can invent a slogan like "Even your best friend won't tell you," which enabled a company to sell millions of bottles of a product to people who did not have the ailment in question—a product which, by the way, wouldn't cure the ailment if they had it.

It is not enough that Mr. Reeves is willing to devote his life to this sort of thing. He is convinced that this is the most worthwhile manner in which a man can hope to pass his mature life. The advertising man, to Mr. Reeves, is "creative"; his efforts to outguess the public are "research"; the man who first jotted down the immortal words "Stop B.O." is a "pioneer."

There is one point made by Mr. Reeves which is valid, and because it is valid it is troubling. A great many useful and serviceable products would not be generally available if it were not for the impetus that advertising has given them. Certain goods stand or fall upon their ability to move quickly into the mass market, and there is no other way than advertising to make an impression on a mass market. And if one advertises, one has the right to expect that the advertising agency will get you a run for your money. It is not the business of the ad man to judge the worth of a product: that is up to the consumer. The ad man's job is to sell it, and if he is an honest ad man, he does it the best way he knows how. But this does not make him a hero. A man is not necessarily ennobled simply because he has been able to sell laxatives to people who don't need them, but who will after they have taken them for a while.

All I ask of Mr. Reeves and his fellows is a little humility. It needn't be much. When they chuckle over the success of a cigarette campaign, let them merely entertain for a moment or two the possibility that they may have helped shorten the lives of a great many people, and that doctors who worry about the link between cigarettes and cancer may conceivably be right. When they write dentifrice ads, and promise miracles out of a compound of soap, air, and flavoring matter, let them wonder briefly how many people will buy the toothpaste instead of seeing a dentist. They would be very nice people if they could only get it out of their heads that a "successful" advertising campaign is a contribution to art, science, and human welfare.

Meanwhile, as it happens, my own sister is happily married, and I have no direct stake in the matter. But I would advise bachelors among advertising men to urge that Mr. Reeves forego the pleasures of publication for a while. He is doing their cause no good.

STEPHEN WHITE

THE INNOCENT EYE OF A MAN OF GALILEE

Late in the fifteenth century the town of Safed, high in the hills of Galilee, was a haven for Jews expelled from Spain under the Inquisition; there they established a center of Cabalistic learning. Today Safed still serves as a haven—mainly for tourists but also for artists, who flock there for the climate and natural setting, the beauty of the old quarter, and the studios the town until recently provided them at nominal rent. Yet of the scores of painters who have made Safed their home, none is so remarkable as a native who has lived there for more than seventy years and is familiar to young and old as "Shalom the Watchmaker." Few of his neighbors know that Shalom Moskovitz paints at all, much less that he has had a one-man exhibit in New York and is becoming known in America as "the Grandma Moses of Israel."

Shalom of Safed

Shalom, like his American counterpart, came late to painting. For more than half a century he worked at various crafts—mainly watchmaking, but also as a stonemason and silversmith—and led a quiet, deeply religious life. Devoted to children, he spent his spare moments fashioning plywood toys, which he decorated with crayons. One day about six years ago, having made a bird of paradise and wishing to give it some brilliant coloring, he asked his neighbor, a painter, for a few brush-dips. The neighbor watched him color the bird and urged him to paint something on paper. Surprised at the thought, Shalom asked, "What shall I paint?" But he took home a few paints and brushes and soon began setting down the subjects closest to his heart—the events of Jewish history, as narrated in the Old Testament and elaborated in the Talmud and other books.

Gradually there accumulated, painted as a private exercise, a sheaf of delightful temperas and oils, from which HORIZON has chosen the seven reproduced on the following pages. In them Shalom, who considers himself a "historical writer" rather than an artist, retells stories from Genesis and Exodus. He follows his texts closely, inserting Scriptural verses and other legends to ensure clarity. His paintings often "read" like Hebrew, with movement and sequence running from right to left and from top to bottom; an example is the last work in this portfolio, which shows Noah and his sons and their wives gathering figs before leading the chosen pairs of animals into the Ark. Shalom also graphically follows geography and religious symbolism: his Israelites always "ascend" to Jerusalem and "descend" into Egypt.

"I am a serious man," Shalom says. "I do not work from my imagination." Yet there is humor in his art—for instance, in his depiction of the slaughter of the firstborn he allows one of the beasts to escape alive (opposite, near left)—and imagination, too, in his vivid colors and arrangement of the elements of his Bible stories. But, most of all, there is in his paintings an irresistible freshness, gaiety, and warmth, the products of a profound innocence. To Shalom the men and events of the Old Testament are as real and vital as those of his own Safed; indeed, there is no distinction in his works between past and present. The firstborn of Egypt are smitten among row houses that might be the new developments built in Safed for immigrants, while a modern steamship (with sail added for good measure) plies the Biblical Nile. Moses, carrying the tablets inscribed with the Ten Commandments, descends from his fiery encounter with the Lord atop Mount Sinai (in the second painting in this group) wearing what look like Bermuda shorts. The Tower of Babel, as Shalom sees it, is built of modern, machine-squared bricks.

Although a "primitive" in the sense of being untaught, Shalom paints neither as a recluse or a total *naïf*: he has traveled as far as Australia, and visits regularly in Tel Aviv. It is the direct and intimate awareness of his heritage that enables him to transcend conventional barriers and forms. As he expresses it, "Truly it is good when your hands can do what your eyes see and you understand."

The Lord smites the firstborn of Egypt, both men and beasts (Exodus 12). At bottom are the Egyptian harvest and the Nile

Moses descends from Mount Sinai, which quakes and flames with the Lord's presence, to his people waiting below (Exodus 19–32)

Adam and Eve eat from the Tree of Knowledge, cover themselves, and are expelled from the Garden of Eden (Genesis 3)

Abraham and Lot, with their possessions, set out from Haran (top right) for the promised land of Canaan (Genesis 12)

זה לוט

Wearing his coat of many colors, Joseph relates his dreams to his father Jacob and his jealous brothers (Genesis 37)

From the top of the Tower of Babel (or Babylon, seen at its foot) the Lord confounds the tongues of men (Genesis 11)

Noah, his sons, and their wives lead the birds and beasts (in pairs but for a single elephant) into the Ark (Genesis 6–7)

**PUBLIC LIBRARY
KANSAS CITY
MO**

DATE DUE			
AUG 20 '46 01			
SEP 3 '46 02			
OCT 30 '46 234			
NOV 27			
MAR 31			
MA 28 '47 60			
AUG 4 '47 38			
OCT 4 '47 64			
AUG 6 '48 14 98			
AUG 23 '50			
FEB 21 '51 73			
JAN 23 '52 37			
SEP 7 '53 T-32			

Stephen Foster

Songs for Boys and Girls

Selected and Edited by

Ella Herbert Bartlett

Specially Arranged and
Simplified for Young People by

Mario Agnolucci

Illustrated by

Stephen J. Voorhies

WHITTLESEY HOUSE

McGRAW-HILL BOOK COMPANY, INC.

New York • London

STEPHEN FOSTER SONGS FOR BOYS AND GIRLS

The spelling, capitalization, and punctuation used in the words of the songs, including the titles, are the same as those in the original editions of the songs, and the musical arrangements follow the original music as closely as possible.

PUBLISHED BY WHITTLESEY HOUSE
A division of the McGraw-Hill Book Company, Inc.

Lithographed in the United States of America

Contents

STEPHEN COLLINS FOSTER was born in Lawrenceville, Pennsylvania, near Pittsburgh, on July 4, 1826. His father was William Barclay Foster, a leading citizen of the community and a member of the Pennsylvania State Legislature, and his mother was Eliza Clayland Tomlinson, whose family was prominent in both Delaware and Maryland. Stephen was the youngest of seven children; his sisters were Charlotte, who was sixteen when Stephen was born, Ann Eliza, who was fourteen, and Henrietta, seven, and his brothers were Henry, ten, Dunning, five, and Morrison, three.

The Fosters were a typical American family which did its share in the development of this great country. Stephen's great-grandfather, Alexander Foster, came here from Londonderry, Ireland, about 1730 and settled in Lancaster County, Pennsylvania. His grandfather, James Foster, fought during the seven long years of the American Revolution and was at Yorktown when Lord Cornwallis surrendered. His father was a quartermaster in the United States Army during the War of 1812. With this background, it seems singularly appropriate that Stephen should have been born on the fiftieth birthday of our republic.

Stephen's boyhood was a very happy one. The Foster home was the center where all the children and their many friends gathered to play games, sing, and listen to the tales of both history and story which Mrs. Foster told so well. Circumstances made it necessary for the Fosters to move several times, but each new house was "home" to Stephen and the one place he had rather be, above all others. No matter where Stephen traveled in later life, he never forgot his home. We find him returning to it and singing about it in his songs, whenever he could.

Unfortunately, Stephen did not like school. He liked children and being with them, but to be in school made him very unhappy, so his earliest lessons were those which he learned at home, usually taught to him by his mother. Music was the only subject that really interested him, and in this he was self-taught.

There is a legend that, at the age of seven, Stephen saw a flageolet (which is a small wood-wind instrument not unlike a clarinet) in a music store and, picking it up, taught himself to play it in ten minutes. Soon after, he was given a flute, which became his favorite instrument. He would amuse himself by the hour playing the popular tunes of his day and picking out combinations of notes which were to become new tunes, many of which we sing today.

When Stephen was fourteen, his father felt that he should have a more thorough education than he could acquire at home. The academy at Athens, Pennsylvania, was known to be a fine school with homelike surroundings. Stephen was entered there, but he was so homesick he had to leave "that lonesome place," at the end of his first term. He could not study, and had he not had his beloved flute to comfort him he could not have stayed as long as he did.

It was while attending the Athens Academy that he did his first composing. The composition was for four flutes, and he named it *The Tioga Waltz.* It was performed by Stephen and three of his classmates at the graduation exercises of the Academy on April 1, 1841. The following year, when Stephen was but fifteen, his first song was published, *Open Thy Lattice Love.*

For the next five years, Stephen lived at home in Pittsburgh. He studied mathematics with a Mr. Moody, and some French and German with another friend. Through his language teacher he met Mr. Henry Kleber, a musician and teacher who lent him some books about music and helped him with the piano. He enjoyed all of this and made great progress, for he was very happy.

During this time Stephen and his brother "Mit" went to see a performance of Christy's Minstrels. Minstrel shows were fairly new then but they became the most popular form of entertainment in America. They were good clean fun, with lots of singing and dancing. The songs were swinging melodies, with fast banjo accompaniment and funny words. The songs appealed to Stephen, and because he liked them he found he could write this type of song very easily. He wrote *Oh! Susanna* and *Old Uncle Ned,* which were immediately popular.

Stephen enjoyed writing songs and he enjoyed the increasing popularity that came with each new composition. However, for one to make his life work that of writing songs did not seem the proper thing, so, when he was nearing twenty-one, he accepted a position as bookkeeper in his brother Dunning's company, Irwin and Foster, in Cincinnati. During his free hours there he wrote many songs, among them *Camptown Races, Nelly Bly, The Glendy Burk, Lou'sianna Belle.*

It was to be expected that the routine work of bookkeeping would become irksome, for music had become his life. His songs were being published and he was receiving more money from them than he was being paid for keeping books. Therefore, he reasoned, music could support him. So, against the judgment of his family, he decided to leave Cincinnati and devote himself entirely to music.

Returning in 1850 to his father's home in Pittsburgh, he applied himself earnestly to his chosen profession. There seemed to be a waiting demand for whatever he wrote, for each new song was better than those that had been written before. Stephen had developed a form of expression, one of haunting pathos, which gave his songs a quality and distinction that set them apart from those of other composers. During this first year after his return he wrote fifteen songs and one piano composition. This was the year in which he composed *Old Folks at Home*, generally considered the best song of all he wrote.

This same year, Stephen Foster married Miss Jane Denny McDowell, a childhood sweetheart. Their married life was not so happy as we all would have wished for them. Stephen's love for his music and his carefree disposition sometimes caused understandable misunderstandings. In 1864, the most tragic figure in American music died alone in New York City. He has occupied a unique position in music ever since and will continue to occupy it, for his immortal melodies are a distinct contribution to the world's music.

Stephen Foster wrote more than two hundred songs. The greater part of these were written between the ages of twenty and thirty. Fortunately, not all his songs were "minstrel songs," although the majority were. An unusual feature of his work is that he wrote the words as well as the music for nearly all his songs. One notable exception to this rule is his delightful *Oh! There's No Such Girl as Mine!* The words of this song were adapted from a poem written by my great-grandfather, Samuel Lover.

In this collection of Stephen Foster songs, I have included songs which in their simplicity, melody, and poetic lyrics show that they were written for children, such as *What Must a Fairy's Dream Be?*, *Slumber My Darling*, and *Fairy-Belle.* I have included another group—*Nelly Bly*, *Some Folks*, *Happy Hours at Home*—which are songs that will be deeply appreciated by young people, and there is a group of minstrel songs which always delight. I have also included four songs which, while they cannot be grouped as songs for the young, are Foster songs which every boy and girl should know and will wish to know—*Old Folks at Home*, *My Old Kentucky Home*, *Old Dog Tray*, and *Jeanie with the Light Brown Hair*. This collection should give one an example of each type of music which has been left us in this rich heritage of Stephen Foster.

ELLA HERBERT BARTLETT.

Camptown Races

Words and Music by S. C. FOSTER.

Mosso
De Camp - town lad - ies sing dis song, Doo - dah!
De long - tail fil - ly and de big black hoss, Doo - dah!
Old mul - ey cow come on de track, Doo - dah!
mp
Doo - dah! De Camp - town race - track five miles long,
Doo - dah! Dey fly de track and dey both cut a - cross,
Doo - dah! De bob - tail fling her o'er his back,

Oh! doo - dah - day! I come down dah wid my hat caved in, Doo - dah! Doo - dah! I go back home wid a pock - et full of tin— Oh! Doo - dah - day!
Oh! doo - dah - day! De blind hoss stick - en in a big mud hole, Doo - dah! Doo - dah! He can't touch bot-tom wid a ten - foot pole, Oh! Doo - dah - day!
Oh! doo - dah - day! Den fly a - long like a rail - road car, Doo - dah! Doo - dah! — Run - nin' a race wid a shoot - in' star, Oh! Doo - dah - day!

CHORUS
mf
Gwine to run all night! Gwine to run all
day! I'll— bet my mon - ey on de
bob - tail nag, some - bo - dy bet on de bay.

Fairy-Belle

Poetry and Music by STEPHEN C. FOSTER

Andante
The pride of the vil-lage and the fair-est in the dell Is the
She sings to the mead-ows and she car-rols to the streams, She
Her soft notes of mel - o - dy a-round me sweet - ly fall, Her
p
legato
queen of my song and her name is Fai - ry - Belle; The
laughs in the sun - light and smiles while in her dreams, Her
eye full of love is now beam - ing on my soul, The

sound of her light step may be heard up - on the hill Like the
hair like the this - tle - down is bourn up - on the air, And her
sound of that gen - tle voice, the glance of that eye, Sur-
fall of the snow - drop or the drip - ping of the rill.
heart like the hum-ming - bird's is free from ev - 'ry care.
round me with rap-ture that no oth - er heart could sigh.
CHORUS
Fai - ry - Belle, gen - tle Fai - ry-Belle, The
mf

star of the night and the lil - y of the day,
Fai - ry - Belle, The queen of all the dell,
Long may she re - vel on her bright sun - ny way.

Some Folks

Written and Composed by S. C. Foster

Allegretto
mp
Some folks like to sigh,
Some folks fear to smile,
Some folks fret and scold,
Some folks do, Some folks do; Some folks long to
Some folks do, Some folks do; Oth - ers laugh through
Some folks do, Some folks do; They'll soon be dead and

die, But that's not me nor you.
guile, But that's not me nor you.
cold, But that's not me nor you.
CHORUS Con moto
Long live the mer-ry mer-ry heart That laughs by night and day, Like the
f
Queen of Mirth, No mat-ter what some folks say.

Oh! There's No Such Girl as Mine

Words from a poem by SAMUEL LOVER. *Composed by* S. C. FOSTER.

Allegretto
Oh! There's no such girl as mine, In all this wide world round, With her hair of gold so fine, And her
Oh! Her soul in sweet - ness flows, She's gain - er of all hearts, There's a smile where - 'er she goes, And a
She's light to the ban - quet hall, She's balm to the couch of care, When a - round us troub - les fall, She—
mf

voice of sil - ver sound. Her eyes are as black as the
sigh when she de - parts. She's loved by the rich and the
cam - ly takes her share. At home or when far a-
sloe, Her lips in a smile com - bine, Her
poor She's free from all dark de - sign, She's
way, Her vir - tues will ev - er shine, Her
breath is as pure as the snow, There's no such girl as mine!
wel - come at ev - er - y door, There's no such girl as mine!
heart is as op - en as day, There's no such girl as mine!

CHORUS
Oh! There's no such girl as mine, In
all this wide world round, With her hair of gold so
fine And her voice of sil - ver sound.

Slumber My Darling

Written and Composed by STEPHEN C. FOSTER.

Andantino
p
Slum - ber my dar - ling, thy moth - er is near
Slum - ber my dar - ling 'till morn's blush - ing ray
Guard-ing thy dreams from all ter - ror and fear. Sun-light has past and the
Brings to the world the glad tid - ings of day; Fill the dark void with thy

twi-light has gone, Slum-ber my dar-ling, the night's com-ing on.
dream-y de-light Slum-ber, thy moth-er will guard thee to-night.
Sweet vis-ions at-tend thy sleep Fond-est, dear-est to me,
Thy pil-low shall sa-cred be From all out-ward a-larms;
While oth-ers their re-vels keep, I will watch ov-er thee.
Thou, thou art the world to me In thine in-no-cent charms.

CHORUS
Slum - ber my dar - ling, the birds are at rest, The
p
wan-der-ing dews by the flowers are car-ressed, Slum-ber my dar-ling, I'll
rall.
wrap thee up warm, And pray that the an-gels will shield thee from harm.
rall.

What Must a Fairy's Dream Be?

Written and Composed by STEPHEN C. FOSTER.

Moderato
What must a Fai - ry's dream be, Who drinks of the morn - ing dew? Would she think to fly 'till she reach'd the sky And
What must a Fai - ry's dream be, Who sleeps when the Mer - maid sings? Would she rob the night of her jew - els bright, To
What must a Fai - ry's dream be When storms in their an - ger cry? Would she mad - ly chase in the wind's em -brace, The
p dolce

bathe in its lakes of blue?— Or gath - er bright pearls from the
spang - le her silv - 'ry wings?— Rock'd on the wind 'bove the
li - ght - ning gleam - ing by,— Or seize on its flash with a
depths of the sea— What must the dream of a Fai - ry be?
land and the sea, What can the dream of a Fai - ry be?
child - like— glee, What must the dream of a Fai - ry be?

Happy Hours at Home

Poetry and Music by Stephen C. Foster.

Allegretto
I sit me down by my own fire - side When the
I sit me down by my own fire - side Where the
mf
win - ter nights come on, And I calm - ly dream as the
child - ren sport in glee, While the clear young voice of our

dim hours glide, Of man - y pleas - ant scenes now
house - hold pride Makes mel - o - dy that's dear to
gone; Of our health - ful plays in my school - boy days, That can
me. And by ev - 'ry art that can charm the heart, They a -
ne - ver come a - gain; Of our sum - mer joys and our
lure my cares a - way, To pre - pare my soul as the

Christ - mas toys, And— ram - bles o'er the stream - let and plain.
swift hours roll, For the du - ties of the bright com - ing day.
CHORUS
Hap-py hours at home! Hap-py hours at home! How the
mf
mo-ments glide by the bright fire-side, In the hap - py hours at home.

Oh! Susanna

Allegretto
I—— came from Al - a - ba - ma wid my
I—— had a dream de od - der night When
I—— soon will be in New Or - leans, And
mf
staccato
ban - jo on my knee, I'm— gwan to Lou - si -
eb - ery ting was still; I—— thought I saw Sus -
den I'll look all round, And— when I find Sus -

a - na, My— true love for to see, It—
an - na, A— - com - ing down de hill. The—
an - na, I'll— fall up - on the ground. But—
rain'd all night the day I left, The
buck - wheat cake war in her mouth, The
if I do not find her, Dis dar -
weath - er it was dry, The sun so hot I
tear was in her eye, Says I, I'm com - ing
kie - 'll sure - ly die, And when I'm dead and

frose to death, Sus - an - na, don't you cry.
from de South, Sus - an - na, don't you cry.
bur - ied, Sus - an - na, don't you cry.
CHORUS
Oh! Sus - an - na, Oh! don't you cry for me, I've
f
come from Al - a - ba - ma wid mi ban - jo on my knee.

Nelly Bly

Words and Music by S. C. Foster.

Moderato
Nel - ly Bly! Nel - ly Bly! bring de broom a - long, We'll sweep de kit - chen clean, my dear, and hab a lit - tle song.
Nel - ly Bly hab a voice like de tur - tle dove, I hears it in de mead - ow and I hears it in de grove.
Nel - ly Bly shuts her eye when she goes to sleep. And when she wak - ens up a - gain her eye - balls 'gin to peep.
mp scherzando

Poke de wood, my la - dy lub, and make de fire — burn, And
Nel - ly Bly hab a heart warm — as a cup ob tea, And
Way she walks, she lifts her foot, and den she brings it down, And
while I take de ban - jo down, Just gib de mush a turn.
big - ger dan de sweet po - ta - to down in Ten - nes - see.
when it lights der's mus - ic dah in dat part of de town.
CHORUS
Heigh! Nel - ly, Ho! Nel - ly, lis - ten lub to me, I'll

sing for you, play for you, a dul - cem mel - o - dy,——
Heigh! Nel - ly, Ho! Nel - ly, lis - ten lub to me, I'll
sing for you, play for you, a dul - cem mel - o - dy.

Ring, Ring de Banjo!

Words and Music by Stephen C. Foster.

Moderato
De time is neb - ber drear - y . If de
Oh! nev - er count de bub - bles While dere's
My love, I'll have to leave you While de
p
dark - ey neb - ber groans; De la - dies neb - ber
wa - ter in de spring. De dark - y have no
riv - er's run - ning high: But I ne'er can de -

wea - ry wid de rat - tle ob de bones: Den
trou - bles While he's got dis song to sing. De
ceive you, So don't you wipe yo' eye. I'se
come a - gain Su - san - na By de
beau - ties of cre - a - tion Will nev -
gwine to make some mon - ey; But I'll
gas - light ob de moon; We'll tum de old pi -
er lose dere charm, While I roam de old plan -
come an - oth - er day, I'll come a - gain, my

an - o when de ban - jo's out ob tune.
ta - tion Wid my true love on my arm.
hon - ey, If I have to work my way.
CHORUS
Ring, ring de ban - jo! I like dat good old song,
mf
Come a - gain my true lub, Oh! wha you been so long?

Jeanie with the Light Brown Hair

Poetry and Music by STEPHEN C. FOSTER.

Andante moderato
mp
I dream of Jean - ie with the light brown hair,
I long for Jean - ie with the day dawn smile,
I sigh for Jean - ie, but her light form strayed
Borne, like a va - por, on the sum-mer air; I see her trip - ping where the
Ra - diant in glad - ness, warm with win-ning guile; I hear her mel - o - dies, like
Far from the fond hearts 'round her na - tive glade; Her smiles have van - ished and her

bright streams play, Hap-py as the dai-sies that dance on her way.
joys gone by, Sigh-ing 'round my heart o'er the fond hopes that die:
sweet songs flown, Flit-ting like the dreams that have cheered us and gone.
Ma-ny were the wild notes her mer-ry voice would pour,
Sigh-ing like the night wind and sob-bing like the rain,
Now the nod-ding wild flow'rs may with-er on the shore
Ma-ny were the blithe birds that war-bled them o'er: I
Wail-ing for the lost one that comes not a-gain: I
While her gen-tle fin-gers will cull them no more: I

dream of Jean - ie with the light brown hair,
long for Jean - ie and my heart bows low,
sigh for Jean - ie with the light brown hair,
Float - ing, like a va - por, on the soft sum - mer air.
Nev - er - more to find her where the bright wa - ters flow.
Float - ing, like a va - por, on the soft sum - mer air.
rall.

Old Folks at Home

Andante
Way down u - pon the Swa - nee rib - ber, Far, far a -
All round de lit - tle farm I wan-dered When I was
One lit - tle hut a - mong de bush - es, One dat I
mp sempre legato
way, Dere's wha my heart is turn - ing eb - ber,
young, Den ma - ny hap - py days I squan-dered,
love, Still sad - ly to my mem - 'ry rush - es,

Dere's wha de old folks stay. All up and down de
Ma - ny de songs I sung. When I was play - ing
No mat - ter where I rove. When will I see de
whole cre - a - tion, Sad - ly I roam, Still long -ing for de
wid my brud - der Hap - py was I Oh! take me to my
bees a - hum-ming All round de comb? When will I hear de
old plan - ta - tion, And for de old folks at home.
kind old mud - der, Dere let me live and die.
ban - jo tum -ming Down in my good old home?

CHORUS
All de world am sad and drear - y,
Eb - ry where I roam,
Oh! dark - eys how my
heart grows wear - y
Far from de old folks at home.
mf
mp

My Old Kentucky Home

Words and Music by STEPHEN C. FOSTER.

Moderato non troppo
The sun shines bright in the old Ken-tuck - y home, 'Tis
They hunt no more for the pos - sum and the coon On the
sum-mer, the dark - ies are gay, The corn top's ripe and the
mead-ow, the hill and the shore. They sing no more by the

mead-ow's in the bloom While the birds make mu-sic all the day. The
glim-mer of the moon, On the bench by the old ca - bin door. The
young folks roll on the lit - tle ca - bin floor, All
day goes by like a shad - ow o'er the heart, With
mer - ry, all hap - py and bright: By'n by Hard Times come a -
sor - row where all was de - light: The time has come when the

knock-ing at the door, Then my old Ken-tuck-y Home, good night!
dark-ies have to part, Then my old Ken-tuck-y Home, good night!
CHORUS
Weep no more, my la-dy, Oh! weep no more to-day! We will
mf
sing one song for the old Ken-tuck-y Home, For the old Ken-tuck-y Home, far a-way.

Old Dog Tray

Stephen C. Foster.

Allegretto
The morn of life is past, And eve - ning comes at last; It brings me a dream of a
The forms I called my own Have van -ished one by one, The loved ones, the dear ones have
When thoughts re - call the past, His eyes are on me cast, I know that he feels what my
mp

once hap - py day, Of mer - ry forms I've seen Up -
all passed a - way; Their ha - py smiles have flown, Their
break-ing heart would say; Al - though he can - not speak, I'll
on the vil - lage green, Sport - ing with my old dog Tray.
gen - tle voic - es gone, I've noth - ing left but old dog Tray.
vain - ly, vain - ly seek A bet - ter friend than old dog Tray.
CHORUS
Old Dog Tray's ev - er faith - ful Grief can - not drive him a -
mf

way, He's gen - tle, he is kind; I'll
nev - er, nev - er find A bet - ter friend than Old Dog Tray.